Staging a Pantomime

Staging a Pantomime

Gill Davies

A & C Black · London

Published in 1995
A & C Black (Publishers) Ltd
35 Bedford Row
London WC1R 4 JH

© 1995 text Gill Davies, illustrations David Playne,
photographs Gill Davies and David Playne

ISBN 0-7136-4120-7

A CIP catalogue record for this book
is available from the British Library.

Typeset in 10/11.5pt Palatino
Designed by Janet Watson
Printed and bound in the United Kingdom
by Butler and Tanner, Frome, Somerset

Contents

Introduction 7

1 Finding a script 8

2 Auditions: casting without tears 15

3 Planning ahead 22

4 The backstage team 34

5 Rehearsals: mob control 52

6 Acting tips and techniques 70

7 Music, dance and crowd scenes 79

8 Audience participation 86

9 Publicity and printed matter 93

10 Children – on and off the stage 103

11 Stock characters and story lines 108

12 The opening night and aftermath 116

13 Practical matters 122

Bibliography and further reading 141

Index 142

Facts from the past
Did you know that . . .

. . . Emperor Nero had his favourite pantomime performer put to death because he was so jealous of his skills.

. . . Pantomime began nearly two and a half thousand years ago in Ancient Rome. Then it was a 'one-man show' – without conventional dialogue but with a chorus backing. The actor used masks to help interpret all the characters in the story.

. . . The first ever recorded pantomime performer, in 467 BC, was a dancer, Telestes.

. . . The tradition of 'goodies' entering stage right and 'baddies' stage left derives from medieval mystery plays when the entrances to Heaven and Hell were placed on these sides.

. . . The original English pantomimes were performed as 'after-pieces', following more serious theatre productions. Available at a reduced rate, they were geared to the working classes who could not escape from their employment in time for the serious stuff. So pantomime inevitably developed as popular entertainment - 'lowering the tone' some protested.

. . . In England and France in the eighteenth century only Theatres Royal were licensed to put on plays with spoken dialogue, so, ever resourceful, the entertainers of the day presented silent pantomime interpretation of melodrama, spectacles and adventures, with notice boards or scrolls to explain the niceties of the plot. These became the most popular form of entertainment.

. . . Dandino in *Cinderella* was drawn from a character in a Rossini opera.

. . . The name Dame Twankey in *Aladdin* was taken from the word 'twankay' – a cargo that was raced home in tea-clippers from the East in the 1860s.

. . . In *Red Riding Hood* the idea of an upright demon wolf (rather than an animal on all fours) was extracted from a contemporary Paris opera.

. . . The word 'slapstick' derives from a wooden bat, shaped like a sword, devised to create the maximum amount of noise while administering the minimum amount of injury as it was used to wallop fellow knockabout actors. Sometimes the slapstick had a split or cleft down the middle to amplify the sound - in the 19th century, gunpowder was inserted in this cleft to add to the effect!

. . . Joe Grimaldi (1802-1832), one of the world's most famous clowns, made his stage debut dancing at the age of two. He devised the make-up which became the basic clown's white face and staged elaborate fairy-tale fantasies written in rhyming couplets. He was so popular he used to appear at Sadlers Wells theatre and then run the three miles to Covent Garden in time for a performance there. Grimaldi never appeared in the circus ring, only in the theatre but his name became a synonym for clown, a 'Joey'.

. . . Lupino Lane (1892-1959), an acrobatic tumbler (descended from an Italian puppet-maker) refined the art of pantomime slapstick. He introduced his fencing, boxing, elocution, ballet, tap and juggling skills to slapstick sketches and devised intricate stage machinery and trick scenery.

. . . 16th-century Italian *commedia dell'arte* strolling players developed a body language that could be understood internationally. Pantomime characters such as Harlequin, Scaramouch and Columbine were involved in an endless variety of situations and adventures - probably the first ever long-running 'situation comedy'.

Introduction

Not to like pantomime is not to like love, not to take a holiday, not to remember we have been children ourselves.

Leigh Hunt

As winter takes its grip, generally in the aftermath of the Christmas festivities, villages, towns, colleges, schools, amateur societies, groups of friends and professional theatres muster forces to put on a show. For this is pantomime season when fairy tales are enacted by actors, dancers, singers and clowns, with all the traditional drama and buffoonery. Ostensibly these are performances to entertain children but adults thoroughly enjoy their magic too.

Few forms of theatre can be more steeped in tradition than pantomime: it is a strange mix of ancient Roman, Italian commedia dell'arte, spectacle, circus, vaudeville and music hall, fairy tale and fantasy, with a hint of the medieval mystery play thrown in for good measure.

Although it has mutated over the years – and continues to do so – pantomime still relies on audience acceptance and understanding of its traditions, on the assumption that every generation of parents will at some stage take their children to a pantomime and show them how to join in. In this way, succeeding generations pass on one of the few twentieth century oral traditions through their audience participation with all those 'Look out behind you!'s and 'Oh yes, you did!'s.

For many, pantomime will be their first experience of live theatre; it may be their only one, so it especially important that every member of the audience enjoys a great show and takes away lasting memories.

Above all, pantomime ought to be fun – fun for the performers and fun for the audience. In fact, this word keeps cropping up time and again in *Staging a Pantomime*. I hope it will be similarly spread through any performances that may be inspired by the reading of this book.

1

Finding a script

The script is the starting point, the source of inspiration for the whole production. If the producer, cast and audience are to enjoy the eventual production, it is vital that the play has their united enthusiasm and support. Of course actors – and audience – can have a whale of a time sniggering over a script they think hilariously dreadful but, in the main, one assumes that the intention is to put on a production that is as good as it can be, in all respects.

There are two main options: to buy a published script that is available for amateur production, or to write your own. As a compromise, you might perhaps borrow a script originated by another drama group.

Who chooses the play?

Generally the selection of the play is the lot of the producer. This makes sense since it is upon his or her energy and enthusiasm for the production that the success of the end product will depend. A single play or a short-list may be suggested. Sometimes the drama society as a whole, or a smaller committee representing them, may make the choice. Certainly they need to support the decision, even if it is not initially theirs. A producer may then be invited to take the production forward, after the committee has made its choice. Or various producers may put forward potential plays, from which one play and producer will ultimately be selected.

What are you looking for?

What kind of play?

Since this book presupposes that the script is a pantomime or something similar, the type of play to be chosen is already a foregone conclusion. However, there are still some decisions to be taken, bearing in mind the kind of audience the group want or expect to entertain and the practical limitations such as size of cast and budget.

Obviously, styles of writing and the contents and demands of different scripts vary. For example, the earliest true English pantomimes were written in rhyming couplets and occasionally pantomimes will retain this style, especially for the more formal speeches such as the villain declaiming his evil intents to the audience. The pantomime can be unashamedly old-fashioned, or futuristic, tell a conventional fairy story, incorporate characters from *Neighbours* or *Batman*, be aimed purely at children or full of innuendo.

The scripts that are made available for amateur production will be geared to family entertainment, but some pantomimes do include blue material that may be deemed unsuitable for the younger members of an audience. Generally, provided the humour is not offensive or heavily stressed and the jokes can go over the heads of children, this need not present a problem. Any unsuitable humour can be readily omitted. The main aim is to find a script with which everyone will be comfortable.

When reading a play alone, it can be difficult to visualise how it will work in performance. A reading with other members of the team is better but even then the purely visual elements, which will add a lot to the final show, can be overlooked. Don't just skip over the stage directions. Try to 'see' the play as well as listening to it.

Several practical matters will also need to be considered when choosing – or writing – a play. Inevitably there will be certain restrictions, depending on the venue and the size of the group.

Size of cast

The size of the cast is a major consideration. It is not unknown for directors, hell-bent on putting on a play with a larger cast than the society can readily muster, to set off, with a fanatical gleam in the eye, to make up the deficit. Friends and relatives learn to have their excuses ready though, not easily thwarted, the producer will accost strangers in the street or at the bar who may fall loosely within the required age range and sex. In this way, if not arrested in the meantime, the truly dedicated producer may well drum up the necessary extra actors, but it is an exhausting and risky business. It is better to find a play where the list of characters corresponds to the available resources.

However, an apparently large cast list can be misleading. It is not always possible to tell from a résumé of a play how easy it is for characters to be doubled up. An energetic cast can thoroughly enjoy taking several roles. It means less time hanging around during rehearsals and performances. Still, the actors can be stretched only so far. What seems rational in the stop-and-go of interrupted rehearsal may not be practicable when the play speeds up in performance and the costume changes become frenetic as buttons, poppers, zips, hooks and eyes slither through sweaty fingers. Bear in mind the age and temperament of the actors concerned before asking too much of their energies and disposition. I have, on occasions, come across panting and red-faced actors, panicking in a cramped corner of the wings, half strangled by one costume and tangled up in another, clearly suffering from nervous strain and exhaustion with only a few seconds to go before their next entrance.

Sex changes

To help decide if the play will work for you, if the cast list is not already so divided, draw up separate columns for male and female characters and then do the same for the available cast.

One of the problems when the play is being chosen is that it is not always easy to ascertain just who is going to be available to act. People's availability often depends on whether they like the play and the particular part offered to them – so it can be a chicken-and-egg situation. To help strike the right balance and adjust a script to suit the acting force, parts can be subjected to a sex change – especially the peripheral roles. With a few suitable amendments to the script, a housekeeper can become a butler or an old uncle an ancient aunt. In one particular production I remember, the role of a brash egotistical male-chauvinist television compère, supported by two 'dolly birds' was very easily transformed into a feisty American lady with two dishy young men in tow. Interestingly, it took only a few minor changes of line to achieve this result and was actually a lot more fun than the original concept.

Animals and inanimate objects that come to life in a pantomime can, of course, be played by either sex (or both – one at each end). When choosing a play (and when auditioning), such parts should be kept as a separate column.

So, ideally, find a play that matches available cast as closely as possible, but, if you really like a script, look at it carefully before dismissing it. Do not take the cast list at face value – explore all the possibilities. And bear in mind that a larger cast means fewer people will be disappointed by not being given roles.

Always make sure that you also have enough people available to create a strong back stage team.

Hopefully, you will find a play that everyone will enjoy.

Age group

There are plays that include children and those that do not. Again, much depends on the pool of actors and the age-range in your group and whether you have any temperamental actors who refuse to work with 'children and animals'. Children do require a good deal of organising. They will often need extra rehearsals, at an earlier time than the adults; and during performances they need to be kept occupied between their appearances on stage.

Make-up can be used to great effect to add or take away years, but it is helpful if at least some members of the cast bear a passing resemblance to the ages of the characters being enacted.

Music

There are pantomimes with music, song and dance and others that contain little if any musical element. Obviously a complicated musical score requires appropriately skilled interpretation, but do not rule out musical productions without first checking out the available talent. You may be surprised just how many singers and musicians are keeping a low profile in your midst.

Technical considerations

The technical requirements of pantomime production are dealt with in detail in Chapter Thirteen. However, some elements must be considered at this stage, before choosing (and then perhaps adapting) a play.

Obviously, if the whole plot hinges on having a revolving stage and trap doors from which a demon king or fairy appear at frequent intervals – whereas your stage consists of a tiny raised platform or blocks at the end of the village hall – then the script will need to be looked at carefully to see if it can be translated to suit without being emasculated. Similarly, the lighting may present some problems if the society has limited equipment.

Few of these difficulties are insurmountable to an imaginative director and technical team, but they need to be looked at carefully early on in the proceedings so that the necessary work can be launched in good time.

It is a general rule that budget and person hours will be in inverse proportion to each other: if you cannot afford to buy or hire it, you will need to make it. So do not choose a play where the input of energy or cash will be totally out of proportion to resources – and/or anticipated income.

Sources of scripts

For an initial reading, scripts can be borrowed from local libraries. Music and drama specialist libraries can be found in most cities and will offer the widest choice.

Single reading copies of plays can be obtained from companies such as Samuel French who publish plays. Full acting sets can be purchased later and the licence for performance will also need to be cleared, preferably prior to rehearsals so that there is no risk of having to abandon a choice of play after rehearsals are under way. For example, although featured in a publisher's catalogue or available on the library shelves, a play may be abruptly withdrawn from amateur performance if a professional revival is to be staged.

Samuel French publish a guide to their available scripts: *Plays for Performance*. This includes a résumé of the plots, the list of sets and characters involved – with brief descriptions of each – and states the number of male and female parts. It also classifies them according to the type of play – classical, comedy, court-room and so on. Samuel French also publish a comprehensive list of basic pantomimes that allow for the inclusion of local and/or topical material and a personal choice of songs.

The Stage and *Amateur Stage* magazines, published monthly, contain advertisements for scripts, both in their major advertising panels and in the classified ads. NODA (National Operatic and Dramatic Association) at present publish *NODA News* three times a year (soon to be four a year) and is another useful source of information and scripts. Other theatre groups may be approached for advice on scripts and are generally delighted to see their own home-made scripts given another airing.

Writing your own script

If at first this seems a rather overwhelming prospect, the novice author or authors should be cheered by the knowledge that a good many amateur companies do produce their own scripts – very successfully, too.

What are the advantages?

As the treasurer of any amateur society will tell you, it is cheap. If the authors expect no payment for their time and trouble, the society will save both the cost of the books and the licence fee. Newly fledged authors are in fact, generally very flattered to see their pieces performed at all.

The scripts will need to be typed and photocopied, of course, and that must be taken into account and costed as necessary. Creating a totally new script is great fun, once it is under way, and opens up all sorts of opportunities. The play can be tailored to suit the society in all respects. The number and age of characters, the complications of your particular venue and resources – everything discussed so far in this chapter – can be taken into account. Moreover, the play can exploit the advantages of the society and particular strengths within the group.

If the author is, as is most likely, an existing member of the group, these elements will already be familiar to him or her. If not, they should be clearly laid out before the pantomime writing begins. This assessment and definition of resources can be a useful exercise for the familiar member-author too.

How to begin

This is the most difficult part of all. Once a script begins to take shape, the characters have a habit of taking over and the play will suddenly begin to roll along. There are times when you hit a sticky patch in the middle, of course, but generally it is those first few pages that are the most taxing and nerve-racking of all, the time when you think that no worthwhile script will ever emerge this time. It will, of course; have faith in the outcome and then work towards it.

Ideally, take time to gather in suitable material. Always have a notebook with you to jot down ideas, jokes or characters that might be brought into the eventual script. Talk about the concept with other members of the group or your family and get them involved. They will enjoy airing their ideas and laughing at the possibilities the theme or story presents and one good idea can spark off another. Moreover, everybody will feel that they have contributed in some way and are part of the exercise. You will not warm to all the ideas, of course, but it all helps the team to gel. At the end of the preparation period – which might be as long as from the end of one pantomime production to the start of another, there will be a comforting wodge of suggestions upon which to draw.

If the production is to be a straight pantomime, there will be a familiar story line. Borrow fairy story books from the library or your children. Analyse the plot; decide which are the vital elements of the story. Then you will have a basic structure upon which to build the play. For example, *Jack and the Beanstalk* consists, give or take a few variations and frills, of the following:

1. Establishing that Jack and his mother are poor and have to sell cow
2. Going to market
3. Meeting man with beans and exchanging cow for these
4. Mother at home, angry
5. Beanstalk grows; Jack climbs up it
6. At top of beanstalk – Jack meets old woman who explains about his father
7. Giant's wife lets him into castle
8. Giant fee-fie-fo-fumming
9. Jack steals hen
10. Jack steals gold
11. Jack steals harp
12. Chopping down beanstalk

In addition to these basic story elements, it is essential to have a good beginning, an opening scene that sets the mood, and a strong finale. If the audience are given confidence in an enjoyable first few minutes, and at the last are treated to a superb final scene, that is what they are likely to remember most. Not that you can let the rest go hang but, if you can, give them a concentration of excellence at these two points, and at the ends and beginnings of acts.

Bear in mind when planning the flow of scenes that there should be ample opportunity allowed to change sets, especially the more complicated ones. To accommodate this, set some simpler scenes, with fewer characters and props, in front of the curtains or a drop, to allow the scene behind to be dealt with meanwhile.

Having established the skeleton plot, you are free to go off at a tangent occasionally, to introduce your own variations on the theme, such as adding a love story (Jack and Jill?) or a dream sequence (the cow jumps over the moon). The beanstalk might shoot up and down and across to all sorts of places. It could dive down to Australia, for instance ('Fee-Fie-Fo Fum, I smell the blood of an English pom!'). Traditionally the script should include some topical and local humour, so that the particular audience feel involved. One village production of *Cinderella*, went so far as to invite the local postman to deliver the invitation to the ball on stage while the village milkman arrived at the kitchen door with various dairy products. This sort of input can be great fun. But make sure that outsiders in the audience do not feel alienated by the in jokes.

The next step is to create a more detailed breakdown of the story, together with your own new ideas, under each of the skeleton sections. For example:

4. **Mother at home, angry**
   a. Mother Hubbard (Dame) and dog, Fido, await Jack's return
   b. Slapstick scene as Mother H. bakes a pie with whatever she can lay hands upon (flour, screws and nails, spoons, dog bones etc.)
   c. Goes into audience for more ingredients and help
   d. Jack returns and shows Mother beans, explaining how he wants to make fortune and marry princess
   e. Mother throws beans away
   f. Cow arrives back, having run away home to rejoin them
   g. Song to close scene

Now all you have to do is fill in the gaps!

How long should it be?

It can be very difficult to judge how much to write. One of the advantages of creating this outline plot is that it enables the author to keep track of the way the play is developing and to maintain a balance. Obviously, some scenes will be longer than others and need to run their natural course, but if your first act runs for only fifteen minutes and the second lasts three hours, something has gone drastically wrong.

Look at an existing play of suitable length and do a sample word count on a typical scene. Compare it to your own. Once you have written your first play, it will be easier to judge – how many pages on *your* typewriter or word processor at a set line length did it take last year to run from about 7.30 to 10 p.m.? If you are working with a machine or program that incorporates a word count, that will help enormously. As a very rough guide, some 10,000 – 12,000 words will provide a sound script. This count includes all the stage directions within the plot but excludes the list of characters, prop lists, lighting plot and so on. Remember to allow for intervals, music, audience participation and new ideas that will inevitably crop up during rehearsal. If anything, err on the short side rather than running too long and exhausting your audience.

A few more tips

Humour is a vital element of any pantomime. If you are worried that your play is too straight, just let any good cast loose on the play and then capitalise on the laughs that will arise during rehearsal. Write them in!

Try to see the characters up on that stage in your mind's eye. Relax and allow them to develop and the humour usually comes along with them. If you reach a difficult point, don't force the issue. Leave it alone for a while and often the problems will unravel when you are asleep; in the morning you will know exactly what to do.

There is a great temptation to write for specific members of the society and this can be a great advantage. However, the characters often take on a life of their own once your imagination lets them. Also, the person you had in mind originally may not, in audition, turn out to be the best, or may be unavailable or may desperately want to audition for another role entirely. That is the producer's problem. On with the writing. By all means allow the people you know, on and off the stage, to be a source of inspiration.

It is useful to spread the load for the actors. This avoids the problem inherent in many plays where a few characters have vast amounts to do and copious lines to learn, while the rest have scarcely enough action to keep them out of mischief. At the same time, it is important not to confuse the audience. They do need to hang on to a few central characters.

Remember to keep track of peripheral characters so that they are not left standing around for ever with nothing to do or say – and don't forget to write in their exits. It is all too easy to become absorbed in another thread of the plot and then discover in rehearsal that some poor souls are still standing there long after you had mentally written them out of that scene.

Don't be afraid to ask for help. Even if the play is not finished, take it along for the group to read and discuss. After all, the best comedians work in pairs and sharing ideas is a great help. I once worked out the end of a murder plot I was writing by asking everybody else who they thought had done it.

It is impossible to instruct people exactly how to write as everybody's style is different. But there are many books on the subject and useful courses and work-shops available. Watch other productions, read lots of plays and when you are writing, stop every now and then to read your own dialogue aloud to get a better sense of how it will feel for the actor to say those lines and how they will sound to the audience.

A pantomime is a good subject for the beginner playwright because the story lines and characters are already there. The basic plot exists.

The rest is up to you!

2

Auditions: casting without tears

Naive newcomers to a dramatic society possibly labour under the delusion that an audition is a way of finding the *best* person for the part. In the professional theatre, and in some semi-professional amateur societies, this is indeed the case.

However, in most local groups there are other factors to take into account. Perhaps the most important is that the cast must get on as a team. If giving the best person the best part means that the same person gets the leading role every year, there will eventually be grumblings and dissent within the group. So the aim is to achieve the most apt casting possible to create the basis for a thoroughly good production.

Michael Green in his *The Art of Coarse Acting* and the associated one-act plays (essential reading for any would-be actor) points out that, far from being judged on merit, the leading part may well be given to the least suitable actor or actress on account of their being the only person whose living room is large enough to house rehearsals. He claims that many auditions are a total sham and serve only as a palliative to those not in the inner clique which has been meeting in the pub regularly and has already cast the play over pints of beer several weeks before the auditions.

This can happen. And the director is bound to have some preconceived notions about who will play what. The most important thing is to keep these notions under control and not to allow them to dominate the decisions, to be open-minded, to let yourself see other possibilities, to be aware of strengths of feeling underlying the seemingly casual air of those auditioning. 'I'm not worried what I do, really!', properly translated, means, 'I care like hell but I'm not going to admit it for fear of losing face'. So, if you discover that Bill is really desperate to play the Fairy, give him a chance to audition and see how he fares. It may prove an unexpectedly good piece of casting.

This is where the pub can in fact be useful – or, if not the pub, coffee afterwards. Try to find a less formal venue to meet after the audition or reading so that the potential cast can air their views about the play and various roles. They will be far less inhibited about their true feelings once removed from the setting of the audition and it can be useful to absorb some of these titbits of information.

It can also be helpful to ask people to fill in a form about the kind of part they want to play. This can be circulated during the reading or audition and will serve as a handy memory-jogger for the director later, as well as an invaluable list of telephone numbers. Ask for information about the particular roles the actors would like to play as well as general comments about the type and size of roles and whether or not they are willing to help backstage, too. It can be useful to find out the heights of the actors at this stage – an invaluable piece of information later when pairing up couples for chorus work or working out crowd scenes so the larger folk are at the back. See sample blank form on page 21 which can be photocopied for use.

However, not everyone expresses their true ambitions on a publicly shared document and there is nothing like relaxed conversation and a little alcohol to draw out the truth.

It is impossible to please everyone, of course. You cannot cast six people in the same much-desired role or give the lady who weighs twenty stone and has a speech impediment the part of Cinderella. None the less, knowing what people would *really like* to do is a useful guide and can hold quite a few surprises.

Read-throughs

A good audition is the result of careful planning. A haphazard read-through may produce results but it is much better to look at the play and characters very carefully beforehand and decide exactly how you are going to proceed in order to make optimum use of the time – and there is never enough of that!

The more groundwork that is put in before everyone gathers together, the more smoothly the auditions will go. This is vital. A muddled audition is all too easily accused of being unfair.

Moreover, it is first impressions that count most. If the producer appears unfamiliar with the script and out of control even before rehearsals begin, then the play will be off to a very poor start.

The first read-through should be a means of allowing the group – in particular, the potential members of the cast and backstage team – to become familiar with the play.

Hearing the play read aloud also helps the producer to evaluate its strengths and weaknesses, how long it is, whether any cuts are required and where its humour evokes most laughter.

At this stage, all producers will be anxious to discover the general reaction to their 'baby'. What they are hoping is that those involved will enjoy the reading and emerge suitably enthusiastic about the possibilities of the play – dying to get started.

If possible, try to place everyone in a circle or take a position where you can see everyone there and be aware of late arrivals. There is nothing worse than turning up to read or audition and then sitting there in silence all evening.

Do not tell actors too far in advance that they are to read a particular role or section. They will immediately thumb ahead through the script and start practising mentally, oblivious to what is going on around them. When their turn arises, they will have no concept of what has been happening in the play up till that moment and will have lost their place entirely. There is a moment's silence and then the inevitable nudges and hissed interchange begins:

'It's you now!'
'What. . . me?'
'Yes, you.
You're reading King Cole, aren't you?
'Yes, ER, oh, sorry. . . um. . . [frantic rustling of pages]. . . where are we exactly?
'Here!'
'Where?'
[The pages are wrenched from the lost soul and flicked over. Fingers jab at the lines.]
'There!'
'Oh. . . there ! Sorry.'

Meanwhile the rest of the group seethe with frustration and may well start reading the lines ahead, making the cause of the interruption more lost and confused than before.

Audition pieces

For the next reading or stand-up audition, pick out those scenes that best test the ability of the actors to interpret the characters concerned. Try to strike a balance between those scenes demanding flamboyant acting and quieter ones. This will enable you to assess the actors when they are giving full vent to dramatic energy and when they are performing in a controlled and disciplined way.

Copies of one or two pertinent extracts can be handed out beforehand so that contenders can mug them up. During the audition, these sections of script can be repeated several times with different groups of people acting. As these groups take their turn, it will also be important to analyse how the different actors interact. Casting decisions will, in part, depend on both the physical relationship and the chemistry of the pairs and groups of actors who will share the stage with each other. So make sure the selected scenes allow these relationships to be explored in full, too.

Things to watch out for during the auditions

Newcomers will need special attention, so be welcoming but cautious, and watch out for the booby trap.

The booby trap is the actor or actress who auditions brilliantly, has a voice that rings out to the rafters, stands well, acts the part better than you could have dreamed and is utterly charming and delightful offstage too. So what is the snag?

Booby Trap 1 cannot learn lines. No matter how fine the acting ability, the moment the script is put down, disaster strikes. The play grinds to a halt. Booby Trap 1 apologises, mumbles 'sorry', promises to learn them by next week, fails to do so, hangs on to the script with an air of desperation, writes lines all over the body and clothing, comes in at the wrong cue, and generally creates consternation and anxiety among the rest of the cast. The audience may well love this actor but he or she is a producer's nightmare.

Booby Trap 2 never turns up to rehearse, or just often enough to keep you guessing. On these occasions Booby Traps act so well and are so charming that you are persuaded to keep them in the cast. Eventually, Booby Trap 2 has had so many stand-ins during rehearsals that you can scarcely remember who is actually doing the part. The performance at the end of the day may be superlative but it is at the cost of fraught nerves and much wasted time.

So how in auditions do you detect a booby trap? You can't. Cross-questioning never reveals these weaknesses. You can introduce a speech to be learned for the audition but Booby Trap 1s may well be able to mug up a single speech tolerably well and even if they don't it's hard to tell whether the problem is caused by the stress of the audition and will disappear during rehearsals. It is wise, therefore, to restrict the use of newcomers to smaller roles until you have established that they are not booby trap material.

In a small society the producer is probably well aware of what has been achieved so far by those long-term members of the group who come to audition. What the producer may not know is just what that person is really capable of when stretched or given a role that suits particularly well.

Open auditions, when actors can elect to try for a part, may bring some surprises. People may be much better – or worse – than you anticipated. They may choose to audition, sometimes very well, for parts that you might not necessarily have considered suitable or to their taste. Be open-minded at this stage. Do not close any doors or drop hints about the casting which will make it difficult to adjust later on.

Obviously the person's acting ability is one of the major considerations when casting. If the audition pieces have been chosen carefully, these will allow such abilities to be evaluated and compared. It is always amazing how very differently the individual actors will approach a role, bringing in or emphasising a whole variety of characteristics – some of which might not have occurred to the producer previously.

It is not essential for actors to have to learn the audition pieces. It enables them to move more freely than when clutching a script but some familiarity and a chance to study the lines first will suffice and may be better than trying to assess an actor who is worried sick about being word-perfect and therefore unable to relax. Bear in mind that some of those auditioning may be very nervous and will perform far better when cast and accepted than when auditioning.

Learning lines does help those who do not read well to better exhibit their talents. Good acting is not the prerogative of the well-educated and some superb acting ability can be concealed by poor reading. Being nervous about mispronunciation or misinterpretation of the written word can, under pressure, be as crippling as the fear of forgetting lines.

However, suitability for a role depends on more than just acting ability. There will be other factors to take into account.

Physique

Does the actor have the appropriate visual appearance? Is he or she the right height, shape, size, colouring and age for the part? Could make-up and costume sufficiently overcome any deficiencies?

Movement

Does the actor know how to move? Many beginners need guidance on what to do with their hands. There is a tendency to fidget, an inability to keep still that can be very irritating to watch. The audience's eyes will be drawn towards the nervous bobbing up and down, the hands wreathing around all over the place or clasped for dear life behind the back. It may be wise to confine the wrigglers to smaller roles until they have learned how to use their body as well as their voice.

This by no means applies to all newcomers, of course. Some simply sweep on to the stage, first time round, and make the old-timers look like rank amateurs. Sickening for the other actors, but not for the producer, whose life is made far easier by innate ability when it arrives. Grab it and encourage it whenever the chance arises!

Voice

Voice projection is important. There is nothing worse for an audience than straining to hear what is being said and then having to struggle to follow the story line with only half the relevant information understood. Most will give up and switch off mentally, thereby missing nuances of plot, and much of the humour.

The producer, who knows the play inside out, may not be so conscious of this as the listener who is new to the play. So it must be guarded against. Poor audibility has ruined many an otherwise marvellous production.

If, at audition, the actor's voice is inadequate, this can perhaps be corrected during later rehearsals, but it is a factor that should not be disregarded, especially if the part is a giant or demon when the loudness is part of the character.

Voice projection is not the only consideration. The voice has many qualities and can strongly convey character. For example, foreign or regional accents, pitch, softness of speech, a lisp, an upper-crust accent, a 'plum in the mouth', a rasping voice, a whine, a husky sexiness – all these contribute to character, whether they are an actor's natural attribute or contrived for the part. Moreover, while make-up and costume can create the illusion of youth, an older voice is often a dead give-away.

How the teams and pairs gel

All these factors – acting technique, stance, stature, voice and suitability for the part – will not only have to be considered for each individual but also how they work in relationship to the others on the stage. If a pair are total extremes in height, for example, this could work very well for a comedy duo but would be far from ideal for a romantic couple. And two very similar voices can sound rather boring if they are heard together on the stage for long periods.

There are always different groups of characters who appear most often together in a play. These mini teams within the overall cast will need to be able to rehearse comfortably together. There can be personality clashes you might want to avoid – or simply practical considerations, like two of the actors being on incompatible shifts at work so that they are never available on the same night.

Pantomime requirements

In addition to the qualities already discussed, which in the main would apply to all kinds of plays, there are some assets that are especially useful in a pantomime role and for which the producer will be looking in particular.

A good rapport with the audience

There is a good deal of audience participation in a pantomime-style production so it is very useful if the actors, particularly in the main roles, are sufficiently confident and relaxed with the audience for the repartee and banter which is so much a part of the entertainment and which the audience so enjoy. An ability to ad lib is especially useful, in order to capitalise on any unexpected situations that may arise during the performances.

Music

A least some members of the cast should be able to sing well. They will then form a hard core of strong voices and will help enormously to lead the less experienced voices and to make a good overall sound.

If there are already dancers in the group, it is a useful bonus and worth exploiting to the full. However, if not, you could contact a local dance school and see if there are any dancers willing to join your show.

A sense of humour

This is the most vital asset of all. The more natural comics in the production and the greater the pool of humorous ideas that can be tapped, the more amusing and enjoyable the final production will be.

Final decisions

The Society will want to be fair to those who join because they want to act. But if the group is to attract and keep audiences, it is vital that standards are maintained. In pantomime, the finite number of roles is not so critical as in conventional plays and usually can be adjusted to suit the quality of those auditioning. Those who are less experienced or competent can be included in smaller or chorus roles and given a chance to gain experience and confidence.

The invisible actor and late auditions

Certain members may believe their talents are such that they do not actually *need* to audition: sooner or later, the producer will telephone to see if they are available or not this time. Some societies have strict rules regarding audition procedure to prevent this: it causes bad feeling amongst those who have struggled through rain and fog, hired baby-sitters, learned audition pieces, coped with nerve-racking scrutiny, and awaited the result with much frenzied leaping to the telephone and asking all the others, 'Have you heard yet?'

However, if members are unable, for quite genuine reasons, to make the original dates and have told the producer so in advance, then an extra audition may be required. Or, if there is clearly no-one suitable for certain roles at the initial auditions – or someone drops out or turns out to be disastrously ill-suited, the producer may be forced to cast a wider net. But latecomers should still audition – ideally alongside those already cast in the relevant parts.

Announcing the cast

If possible, convey your decisions by letter or telephone - especially to those who will be most grieved. Announcing the cast in front of all and sundry is, at best, uncomfortable for the disappointed and, at worst, humiliating. And even those who have been given parts may feel hampered in their reactions, their pleasure curbed by their consciousness of the disappointed friends in their midst.

With the casting finalised, a most important, and difficult, part of production has been accomplished. Now it is time to appoint the backstage team.

Name What name do you want on the programme?	Height (M / ft)	Role Role preferred Any comments	Backstage Which capacity Abilities	Address including post code	Telephone H for home W for work	Fax H for home W for work
	M / ft					
	M / ft					
	M / ft					
	M / ft					
	M / ft					
	M / ft					
	M / ft					
	M / ft					
	M / ft					
	M / ft					
	M / ft					
	M / ft					

The audition form: this will serve as an invaluable list of names and addresses and as a guide to the interests and inclinations of those who audition. The height factor will help determine pairing and positioning for chorus work.

3

Planning ahead

The casting of the play is settled. The onerous task of telling the unsuccessful aspirants that they are not needed has been dealt with. Now the planning of the production can begin in earnest.

The enthusiastic producer will undoubtedly have been thinking about how he or she visualises the play for a considerable time already, but turning the dreams into reality is another matter altogether. Before rehearsals commence the producer indulges in visions of a smooth-running production with actors interpreting the characters quite beautifully, everyone knowing their lines and then technical genius and wizardry adding to the magic of the presentation. These images are soon to be shattered.

The real world is more likely to be a maelstrom of fraught egos and mounting tension as those dedicated actors who do turn up regularly and entirely share the producer's commitment become increasingly exasperated by the absenteeism and early departure of the other, less perfect souls, or are constantly chastised by their partners back home for spending all their time at rehearsals instead of decorating the spare room.

Even with an entirely dedicated cast, somehow there is never quite enough rehearsal time. You cannot expect to avoid conversations like this:

PRODUCER That was terrible! Look, it really is critical that we get this scene right. The whole play pivots around it. Can you all make an extra rehearsal tomorrow night?
SHEELAGH We can't come tomorrow night. We're in Basingstoke.
KELLY And we're bell-ringing on Tuesday.
LYNNE And I'm on a late shift, anyway.
TONY And I'm playing skittles on Wednesday.
JUNE I suppose I could come on Tuesday, but there's not much point if no one else can.
SHEELAGH We could manage Thursday.
LYNNE AND KELLY Yes, Thursday's all right with us too.
TONY The WI have the hall booked on Thursday.
PRODUCER Ahhhh!

The point is that time is precious and if rehearsals are to be used to the full, the producer needs to be really well organised. There is much that can be done in advance.

The formalities

Make sure these are all in hand so that there are no last-minute panics. There is nothing worse than having to postpone or cancel a play because the fire officer insists on new seating being installed or you discover the licence is unavailable. In an established society there will probably be a committee and an existing system to deal with all the official red tape but for a newly formed group, these procedures will need to be investigated and set into action well in advance.

Booking the hall

It sounds obvious – but it is the kind of thing that everybody can think *someone else* has done. Make sure that not only the dates of the actual performances are booked but also enough time for on-site rehearsal and the erection of the set, as well as the time to clear up afterwards. A party after the Saturday performance can become a Cinderella affair if the hall has to be entirely back to normal by nine the following morning for the local indoor bowls team. And nobody wants to share their Saturday-night performance or their dress rehearsal with the bingo club – so book *all the dates required* as soon as you know them. Some societies, in fact, book the whole set of dates for a season in one go.

Entertainment licence

Performing for a paying audience requires an entertainment licence. If the venue concerned has already been used for such activities, by the local school, for example, then this may already exist, but do ask and find out – and check if there are any specific requirements to be met, such as the correct proportion of toilets for the numbers expected. Your audiences per night may be restricted if your loos are not up to the job. There will, in any case, be a limit on the audience capacity permitted according to the size of the hall.

A seating plan will probably need to be submitted to the local authorities. Aisles will have to be a particular width and exit signs clearly visible, with emergency batteries to keep them glowing if there is a power failure. These should be standard fittings in a commonly used hall.

Insurance

In any public hall, insurance and public liability should be covered already but, again, make sure that the policies are up to date and provide sufficient cover for both the audience and the group – for rehearsals as well as performances.

Fire regulations

These can be quite strict and fire officers are empowered to stop a show mid-performance if they feel the necessary precautions have not been taken. So it is important to make sure you are complying with the requirements.

All the scenery must be fireproofed. This includes tabs and curtaining. Fireproofing crystals can be bought or a mixture made up as follows:

15 ounces (425 grams) of boracic acid crystal
+ 10 ounces (283 grams) of sodium phosphate
in a gallon (4 litres) of water.

Check delicate fabrics first to see if there are any problems with colours running or shrinkage.

Generally, a fire prevention officer will call round and check the venue prior to the performance and will advise on any specific requirements. This officer will not be happy if flammable material is stored under the stage, for example.

Sadly, real candles with their wonderfully atmospheric flickering and shadows will not be permitted. Find out about electric equivalents. Pyrotechnics, such as the various bangs and flashes for Aladdin and his lamp, have to comply with safety regulations too, but special-effects hire companies can advise on this. And you may need a special licence to use a gun – even a starting pistol.

Electricity

Do ensure that the electrical-current supply is adequate to deal with all the lighting equipment that will be used. Special effects and exciting lighting effects may stretch your resources beyond the levels of safety. The Electricity Board will provide an additional supply if necessary.

Food and drink: health regulations and licences

Current legislation imposes a fairly strict regime on the preparation of food for public consumption and, if you wish to serve food in the intervals, it may prove simplest to stick to cold offerings and to prepare everything at home first.

Alcohol can be sold only under licence to adults; a member of the group will need to go to court to obtain this licence, and only so many licences will be available each year to any one group. Alternatively, a local publican might provide a 'casual' licence. In either case, considerable notice is required so set the wheels rolling as soon as the dates are fixed.

Copyright

All published plays are protected by the copyright laws. In certain circumstances, when no charge is being made for admission and the performance is private – with the public excluded – copyright fees may be waived, but this must still be cleared with the publishers prior to the performance. Licences for performance can be obtained from the publishers. Music is protected in the same way and if the music is not an integral part of the play, written specifically for it, licences for performance will need to be obtained from:

The Performing Rights Society Limited
29-33 Berners Street
London W1P 4AA
Telephone 0171-580 5544
Fax 0171-631 4138

Obviously you will also require copies of the play, which will probably need to be ordered from the publishers. Do this in plenty of time, too.

A rehearsal plan

You will need to make the most of the actors' time. This will make for efficient rehearsals and will also avoid bad feeling. Waiting around in a draughty hall for hours on end can be very galling when the actors have gone to some trouble to get there on time. So it is to everybody's benefit to work within a well-organised schedule.

The calendar

First of all, draw up a calendar with all the available rehearsal dates so that all the possible options and permutations can be considered. These dates are the blank spaces into which you will slot the rehearsal times. Make some copies of the blank sheet; it will probably take a few attempts and adjustments before the final rehearsal plan is to everybody's satisfaction.

Check if the rehearsal venue is indeed free at all the times required. Do not assume that it is readily available throughout. Most halls and rooms are used for a variety of purposes by many different groups of people so double-check all the dates. Even if you are meeting in private homes, there are bound to be some clashes.

Try to be clear about dates right from the start. Adjusting a carefully structured schedule is easier at the beginning than it will be later on, since any changes have a knock-on effect.

Moreover, however good your communications, there is always the risk that some misinformed souls will remain blissfully unaware of a changed date or venue and will turn up and find themselves in a skittles match or a choir concert. Accusations will fly and the organiser will be held responsible - even if the fault lies with the actors concerned – so it is wise to make as few changes as possible and to ensure that these are put clearly in writing, not just announced. There will be bad feeling if there is a mix-up – the offenders might even decide that skittles or the choir are more fun than dramatics and never appear at rehearsals again.

With the diary dates listed, start pencilling in the rehearsals. This sounds like odd advice but do not begin at the beginning. Begin your rehearsal schedule at the end and work back. Start with the final dress rehearsal and set that date. Whatever else happens, the performance dates are fixed and the final rehearsals must culminate at that point. Try to leave one clear night between the last rehearsal and the first performance so that everyone can draw breath and renew their energies before the show begins in earnest.

Then decide how many dress rehearsals you actually need. A minimum of two will be required to iron out any problems that arise. Ideally, aim to have at least three full runs in costume, with all the props and scenery changes – if these are ready. How much of the technicalities can be included depends on the availability of the venue before the performances and whether lights and equipment are permanent or being hired at the last minute. Even if the hall is not open to the cast until immediately before the show, run-throughs elsewhere will still enable difficult costume changes to be timed and will help to speed up the technical changes.

An additional advantage is that such rehearsals, especially if set two or three weeks before the performance, spur on the backstage team with their preparations and shock the cast into brushing up their lines. They bring about a sudden awareness on all sides that the play is actually going to happen.

So, with the dress rehearsals fixed, find time for at least one technical rehearsal, two if possible, and then move back in time, slotting into the diary dates all the rehearsals you deem necessary.

Run-throughs

During the last three weeks of rehearsal, it helps to have at least three or four run-throughs, over and above the dress rehearsals. This will help everyone, front- and backstage, to have a proper understanding of the continuity and flow of the play and to appreciate how the timing relates to their particular role.

Polishing rough areas

There are always some problem areas – perhaps because someone has been ill and missed a lot, or had to be replaced, or because a particular section, such as a slapstick scene, is especially complicated. Knowing this to be inevitable, I always try to leave a slot somewhere in the last but one week for the inevitable rough bits that need special attention.

Music and movement

Specific music rehearsals should be dotted throughout the rehearsal schedule and will provide invaluable concentrated attention. This will help with the learning and polishing of songs and with the choreography that is involved – both for small groups of singers and/or dancers and to ease the complications of moving large numbers of people around on the stage for the chorus scenes.

Give every act fair attention

Still moving backwards through the diary, plan when to run complete acts. Ensure that the time is shared fairly so that no one act is neglected. If a particular act is especially complicated, it will need extra rehearsal so the time share may not be equal but must, nevertheless, be correctly balanced. It is embarrassing for an audience to watch a play that begins well but grows progressively worse – a clear sign that rehearsals always began with page one, Act One, and never actually reached Act Three until the last week of rehearsal.

Now jump to the beginning of the rehearsal schedule in your calendar and pop in the first two or three straight rehearsals. These will probably involve the entire cast and aim to familiarise everyone with the play and allow the plotting of moves.

Working in teams

Depending on the structure of the pantomime and how the characters interact, it is generally very useful to divide the cast up into teams, say into four or five groups of people who always tend to appear together. Don't worry if some characters appear in more than one grouping.

This dividing into teams is especially useful in the early stage of rehearsals when the action is 'stop and go back' and much repetition is involved. It is more satisfactory for everyone involved to work within a smaller group in a concentrated way than to be kept hanging around waiting with little or nothing to do because a difficult scene is taking all evening.

For example, in *Jack and the Beanstalk* the teams might be as follows:

Team A

Chorus and dancers	Princess Jill
Peasants	Herald
Townsfolk	Footmen
King Cole	Wedding guests

Team B _____

Jack	Mrs Hubbard
Jill	Buttercup the Cow
Beanseller	Toby the Dog

Team C _____

Jack	Money Bags
Giant	Henrietta Hen
Mrs Dreadful, the Giantess	Singing Harp

Team D _____

Gypsy	(Jack needed occasionally so will
Demon	be included in special C/D nights)
Fairy	

Now chalk in these team rehearsals in appropriate proportions into the remaining slots in the diary.

Other considerations

Nothing in life is simple and certainly not when large numbers of people are involved in a production in their spare time. The rehearsal schedule may have to take into account the cast's particular needs. It is no good calling Team D to rehearse on evenings when Henrietta Hen and the Fairy are both playing darts or are taking part in the pub quiz league. If some of the cast work shifts this needs to be considered somehow, too. However, the permutations can become impossibly complicated if the producer continually falls over backwards to accommodate every other person's problems and whims, so the best ploy is to spread each type of rehearsal (specific teams, acts, run-throughs and music) over a variety of nights and then swop or adapt if there are any major hiccups.

Remember to mark in any committee or backstage meetings to avoid double-booking. And do keep some time free for life at home with the family – for yourself and the cast – so that the likelihood of revolution within the ranks is diminished.

If times and venues are variable, do make it perfectly clear where each rehearsal takes place and at what time it commences so there is no possibility of doubt, error or argument.

Distribution

When the schedule is as ready as it can ever be, hand out copies to all concerned, not forgetting the backstage team. The actors will probably collect theirs at the first rehearsal they attend. Print a reasonable number of extras because some copies *always* go astray.

Telephone tree

When the village hall burns down, a flu epidemic decimates the cast, blizzards and snowdrifts make roads impassable or the pianist has a nervous breakdown, you may need to cancel or postpone a rehearsal at short notice. Phoning every member of the cast and the backstage team can be time-consuming and expensive so share the load by anticipating this event and drawing up a telephone tree, whereby messages of any kind (including happier ones, such as 'It's Jenny's birthday and

REHEARSAL SCHEDULE

THIS IS IT, FOLKS! LET'S MAKE THIS A BLOCKBUSTING/SUPERB SUCCESS. . .To do so, we need good teamwork and your constant support at rehearsals. Please, please, TURN UP ON TIME - and let us know, in advance, if you cannot come - Let's work hard and play hard and have a great time putting together a **GREAT SHOW!**

Team A Chorus and dancers:
Peasants and Townsfolk; Wedding guests
King Cole
Princess Jill
Herald
Footmen

Team B Jack
Princess Jill
Beanseller
Mrs Hubbard
Buttercup the Cow
Toby the Dog

Team C Jack
Giant
Mrs Dreadful, the Giantess
Henrietta Hen
Money Bags and Singing Harp

Team D Gypsy
Fairy
Demon
Henrietta Hen
(Jack occasionally on C/D nights)

JANUARY

Saturday 7 *Hall*
2pm Plot moves *Acts 1 & 2*

Sunday 8 *Hall*
2pm Plot moves *Act 3*
3.30 pm ALL music

Monday 9 *Hall*
7.30pm *Slapstick scene* (p12-14)
8.30pm *Team B*

Friday 13 *Social club*
7.30pm *Team C*
8.45pm *Team D*

Sunday 15 *Social club*
1.45pm *Team A*
3pm *Music - Everyone!*

Monday 16 *Social club*
7.30pm *Team A*

Thursday 19 *Social club*
7.30pm *Team B*
8.30pm *Team C/D*

Friday 20 *Social club*
7.30pm *Team D*
9pm *Music - Everyone!*

Sunday 22 *Social club*
1.45pm *Team A*
2.45pm *Team B*
3.45pm *Team C/D*

Monday 23 *Hall*
7.30pm *Act 1*

Thursday 26 *Hall*
7.30pm *Act 2*

Friday 27 *Social club*
7.30pm *Act 3 scene 1*
8.30pm *Act 3 scene 2 & ALL music*

Sunday 29 *Social club*
1.45pm *Act 1*
2.45pm *Act 2*
3.45pm *Act 3*

Monday 30 *Social club*
7.30pm *Rough areas* (as needed)

FEBRUARY

Thursday 2 *Social club*
7.30pm *Act 2*
8.45pm *Act 3*

Friday 3 *Hall*
7.45pm *Act 1*
9.05pm *ALL MUSIC EVERYONE!*

Sunday 5 *Hall*
2.00pm *RUN THROUGH*

Monday 6 *Hall*
7.30 pm *Act 2*
8.45pm *Act 3*

Wednesday 8 *Hall*
(Bruce away)
8pm *Words rehearsal* EVERYONE
9.30pm *Music & finale* EVERYONE

Friday 10 *Hall*
9.05pm *Act 1*

Saturday 11 *Hall*
Work parties scenery painting

Sunday 12 *Hall*
10 am - 1pm - work parties

Sunday 12 *Hall*
2pm *DRESS REHEARSAL*

Monday 13 *Hall*
7.30pm *Acts 2 & 3*

Thursday 16 *Hall*
7.30pm *RUN THROUGH*

Friday 17 *Hall*
9pm *Music and finale*

Saturday 18 *Hall*
10pm Finish set
6pm *Technical run-through.*
Lighting, sound, props, special effects, stage manager + stage hands

Sunday 19 *Hall*
DRESS REHEARSAL (full) Actors & costumes to arrive 2pm for 2.30 start. Please bring sandwiches in case we need second run-through

Monday 20 *Hall*
6.30pm *DRESS REHEARSAL* (no makeup)

PERFORMANCES
22, 23, 24 and 25 February
Arrive from 6.15 pm
Curtain up 7.30 pm prompt

Friday 24
Producer's party

Saturday 25 *Hall*
Party afterwards - prepare your party pieces now!

Sunday 26
10 am Clearing up the Hall

Rehearsal schedule: this schedule covers six weeks or so of fairly dense rehearsal. After the plotting of moves, the initial rehearsals concentrate on work with smaller teams and on music before 'running' the acts. Venues and times should be clearly stated.

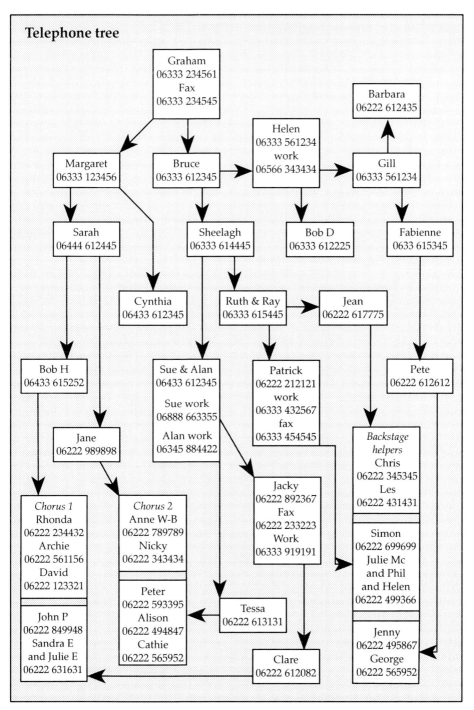

A telephone tree for the dissemination of information, such as a change of venue or time allows messages to be circulated throughout the team with no one person having to make more than, say, two telephone calls.

we're organising a party after the rehearsal tonight – bring a bottle') can be relayed to all concerned.

It can be very useful to ask the person at the end of each line to phone 'head-quarters' and report in when the message has been received. This will enable the organiser to be reassured that there have been no breakdowns along the lines of communication and that everyone concerned has been informed.

To ensure the telephone tree is not lost, make it big and bold on the back of the rehearsal schedule or insist it is attached to play copies.

Plotting moves

Before the cast assemble to commence rehearsals, it is essential to plan the moves. Chaos will reign if no preparatory work has been done, especially when large numbers of people have to be manoeuvred around. Don't keep actors waiting while you hum and haw and change your mind over decisions that could have been taken beforehand. But it is essential to keep an open mind during rehearsals so the moves can be adapted when the action is tried out on stage.

Different producers like to work in different ways. Characters can be represented by coloured pieces of paper, chess pieces or tiddlywinks, and then moved around on a scale drawing of the stage floor plan to enable some first decisions to be made. Do not forget to indicate the positions of furniture, major props and entrances. This will provide only a rough approximation of where the players will move within the acting areas but it is a good starting point. The points of entry and exit and the flow of movement can be thought through to avoid crowding, crossing and collisions.

Once you have experimented with these mobile elements and created a satisfactory pattern of movement, these moves can be superimposed on plans of the stage as lines with arrows, perhaps using a different coloured pen for each character and marking the stationary positions with a circle.

Lighting and sound

Lighting and sound plots will also need to be considered as soon as possible, especially if specific pieces of equipment or recordings have to be ordered or made in advance. The sections on lighting and sound in Chapter Thirteen deal with this in more detail.

The budget

Every production – whether a play in the West End or a village concert – requires some financing or backing. No production can take place without money changing hands, even if only for programmes or coffees in the interval, and it is important to organise this aspect properly and to keep clear records of predicted and actual expenditure for future reference. These records will be invaluable in estimating the costs of future productions.

A newly formed group may have to dip into their own pockets to launch their first pantomime. Once a society is established and has a savings or bank account with the profits from past productions to draw upon, it will be able to finance the initial costs of the production. A pantomime is generally a popular event and the society should be able to sell sufficient tickets for the production to be self-supporting but

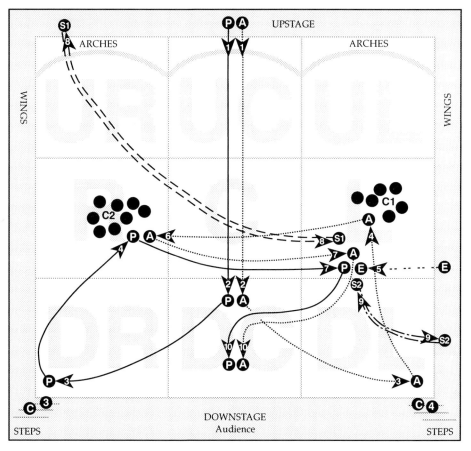

Key

A Aladdin

E Emperor

P Princess

S1 Slave

S2 Second Slave

C1 Crowd
(Lynn & Kelly, David & Gill,
Paul & Jenny)

C2 Crowd
(Miles & Clare, Mark & Sian,
Jim & Sue, Tony & Tessa)

C3 Crowd
(Bob & Julie) ON STEPS DR

C3 Crowd
(Patrick & Viv) ON STEPS DL

Moves

Crowd in pairs, men behind women, arms around
waists, laughing, talking

1 P & A enter *UC* - Crowd cheers

2 P & A move *DC*

3 P & A separate, A to C4, P to C3 - shake hands, kiss etc

4 A to C1, P to C2 - mingle

5 E enters

6 A goes to P

7 A & P to E - bow, receive his blessing on betrothal

8 S1 enters *R* with gifts

9 A & P pass gifts to S2 who exits with them *L*

10 A & P back to *DC*

SONG

*Plotting the moves for the betrothal celebrations in Aladdin. Characters are represented by letters
and the order of moves appears in the arrows. Using a different coloured line for each character
will help to clarify the different paths followed. A blank form for your use is on page 33.*

decisions have to be taken over the prices to be charged to the general public and how to balance the incoming revenue against the outgoing costs incurred. It is still, of course, essential to limit expenditure.

Many societies hope to receive sufficient income from their pantomime productions to fund other less financially rewarding productions. With the play cast and the first rehearsals planned, the people who will be allocating or spending money should be asked how much each of them believes will be needed to fulfil their particular obligations. Draw up an agenda for a budget meeting and discuss the following with all concerned.

Society expenditure and investment

This refers to long-term schemes for the society as a whole and covers those items that may not fall directly within the budget of the individual play, such as building a stage extension, general repairs, new wings or steps, buying a carpet or a first-aid kit, cleaning and fireproofing curtains, installing an intercom system and so on.

Pantomime costs

Licences, insurance, copyright clearance and so on.
Scripts and music scores.
Schedules etc.: typing and photocopies.
Hire of hall and rehearsal rooms.
Costumes: making and hire.
The sets, materials, wood, canvas, paint, nuts and bolts etc.
Lighting and electrics.
Sound.
Special effects.
Properties.
Any prizes or hand-outs to the audience.
Publicity: posters, press advertisements, direct mail and any sundry advance
  information.
Printing: tickets and programmes.
Communications and administration: stamps and telephone calls.
Catering: food, wine, coffee or whatever.
Raffle prizes and tickets.
Make-up and wigs.
Miscellaneous production costs, specific to the play.
After-play parties and entertainment.
Flowers (or equivalent) for the after-play presentations.
Contingency allowance.

Quite a number of these items, such as raffle prizes, typing, parties and telephone calls, may be offered free by members but they should be listed, appreciated and taken into account in case in future years they have to be funded from the budget.

More than one meeting will almost certainly be required to keep track of production expenditure and to reassess the situation as it progresses in case cuts, fund-raising, the tightening (or loosening) of the purse-strings becomes appropriate. It is also very useful to have a post-production meeting when all the bills have been amassed and paid, to evaluate the success or otherwise of the production from a monetary point of view.

Full steam ahead

Now the groundwork has been done. The red tape has been cut through, rehearsals are organised, the moves have been planned, the budget is agreed upon and publicity schemes set in motion. The cast have been chosen and given their scripts to study. The backstage team have been established and have discussed their roles and ideas. Everyone is ready to begin their preparations for an exciting team production.

If the project has been tackled properly, enthusiasm will be running high and the production will be launched in an air of optimism and exhilaration. This is the best possible start for any show.

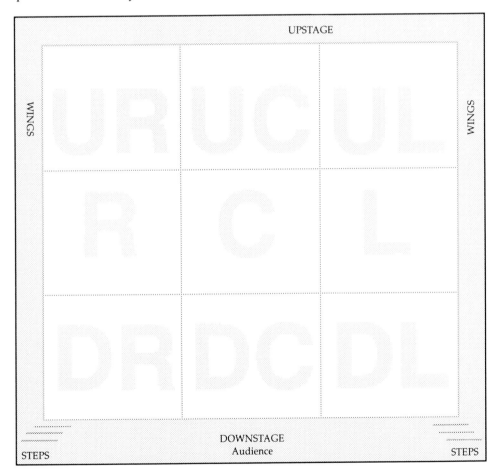

This page has been cleared for copyright and can therefore be photocopied to provide blank stage plans for the plotting of moves in your own pantomime productions, It will need to be adapted if your stage is a different shape and additional factors such as stage extensions should be included.

4

The backstage team

Auditioning and selecting the acting team is often seen as the most crucial decision when launching a play. The calibre of those who are performing is indeed important but the technical backup is an equally significant factor and the polish of the final production will depend upon it. In pantomime, this is particularly important because special effects, complicated costumes, scenery and so on are a prominent part of the package.

Many well-established societies have a backbone of members who are always willing to work behind the scenes. A good number of these workers proclaim they would never dream of appearing on stage but thoroughly enjoy the challenge of helping to create a play – as well as the excellent social life that is generally the bonus of belonging to an amateur dramatic society.

Sometimes, however, it may be necessary to swell the ranks backstage by asking for help from those have not been cast this time. At first, acting members who are asked to help behind the scenes instead of performing may, understandably, see this as second best, but many will later comment how much they have enjoyed the experience.

It is useful to discover at the auditions just who would be willing to contribute behind the scenes if not given the opportunity to act. Not everyone will be happy to give up huge chunks of their time this way, but in general most people enjoy some kind of involvement and are willing to help in order to support the group.

Finding the right skills

It is just as important to match abilities and attitudes to the particular demands of the jobs backstage as it is for front-stage roles. The actual techniques – the making of properties and costumes and how to use lighting, sound, make-up and so on are discussed in Chapter Thirteen so this chapter concentrates on *what* the backstage team are expected to do, rather than *how*. You will need to find suitable people to manage the following jobs:

stage manager	make-up
stage hands	prompt
wardrobe	publicity
properties	creating tickets, posters and programmes
set designer	keeping accounts
set construction and painting	selling tickets
lighting	front of house
electrics	*If required*
sound	catering
special effects	waitresses

Obviously, some of these roles will be doubled up. For example, the electrics might be handled by the lighting person, sound and special effects might come under a single person's jurisdiction, while those involved with set construction and painting often turn into stage hands for the production. None the less, a lot of dedicated people (about fifteen) are required if no one person is to be overloaded. Much depends on the intricacy and scale of the production, the number of scene changes and so on.

I have in the past belonged to small tight-knit societies where the cast have themselves sold all the tickets, painted the sets, made their costumes and done their own make-up while the stage manager, prompt, lighting man and one general assistant did just about everything else. Because there was good discipline and much loyal enthusiasm, this worked out very well but it did claim enormous amounts of energy and time. Even though the cast themselves were sufficiently enthusiastic to give this time, overtiredness takes its toll, and some members of their abandoned families began to protest hotly.

There are different ways to organise a show and producers, while overseeing everything, will want greater input in certain areas than others, depending on which aspects of the production interest them most. As a general rule, the following divisions of labour and responsibility are usual.

A good stage manager

The stage manager is the producer's right-hand man or woman. An experienced and responsible stage manager is a godsend. He or she will organise all the back-stage team and will be totally in charge of operations during the performances.

Often the stage manager will also have been involved on the pre-production construction and set planning, and will be intimate with the function and requirements of the scenes and scenic effects. Certainly he needs to have sat in at the rehearsals and made close note of the director's aims. He is, in effect, the director's deputy and needs to be on the same wavelength. The stage manager needs to exercise discipline *and* diplomacy.

Duties

The stage manager's overall commitment is to control the production from the final dress rehearsal onwards.

Hall keys The stage manager needs to ensure all the necessary keys are available so that everyone can get in on time and that everything is switched off and closed up properly after the performances, unless there is a caretaker who oversees this.

Giving clear orders and direction Communicating with everyone throughout the performances to maximise efficiency and the smooth running of the whole show.

Keeping everyone calm and happy Dealing with any anxieties and arguments and doing his or her best to ensure that no minor quibbles or worries affect the performances.

Giving cues and count-downs Ensuring all the actors are there ready for their cues and at the correct entrances, and giving out suitable warnings of impending cues:

Half an hour to go, folks! Twenty minutes to curtain up! Ten minutes left! Five minutes: overture and beginners, please! Cow – you are on in five minutes! Chorus, it is time for the fairground scene! Gather in the wings in two minutes and quietly, please.

Responsibilities **Pre-production**

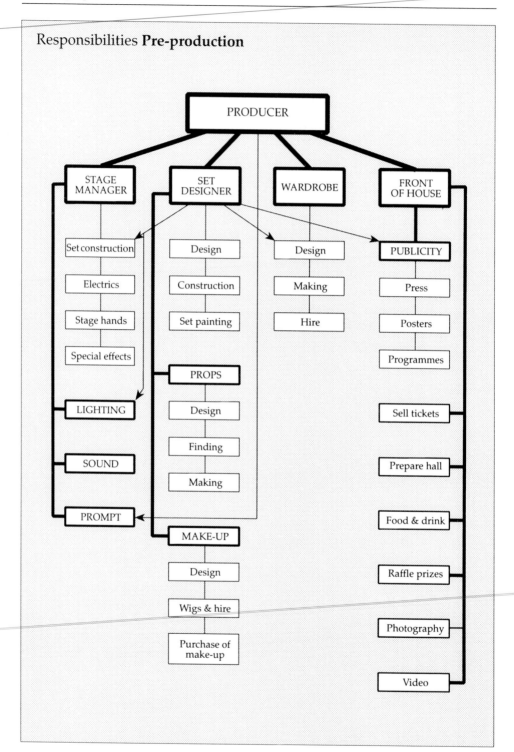

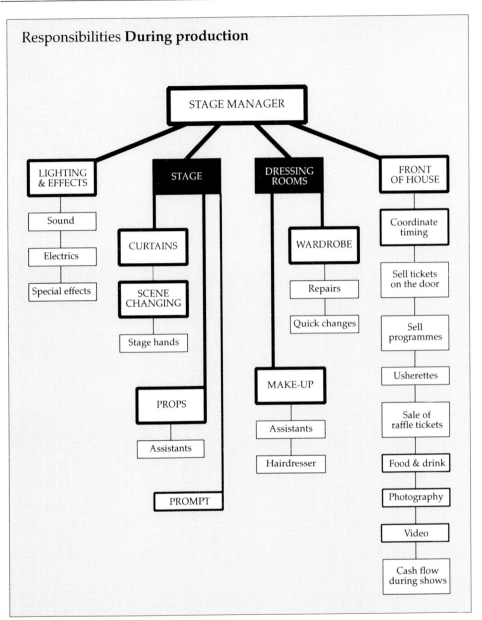

Responsibilities **During production**

Above: During the actual performances the running of the show becomes the responsibility of the stage manager who is helped by the team of backstage experts and assistants. None the less, the producer's influence will still be felt.

Opposite: The producer has to oversee an enormous range of activities during the planning and rehearsal stages of a production. Much of this will be delegated to other experts within the group but it is still ultimately the producer's responsibility, perhaps with the help of a committee, to ensure that all the facets of production are dealt with in a satisfactory manner and suitably complement the style of the pantomime.

Controlling noise levels   Telling everyone to shut up.

Overseeing the scene changes   Making sure everything has been done by the stage hands and is in the right place.

Coordinating all the other backstage elements   Checking sound, lighting, special effects and props to ensure everyone has everything done at the right time, and is ready, especially during scene changes.

Controlling the curtain   Coordinating closely with front of house, musicians and beginners to ensure a well-timed curtain up at the beginning of the show and after each interval. An intercom is useful for this.

Controlling the opening and closing of the curtain and any drops throughout the performances.

Controlling the curtain during the finale and final bows. This must be planned carefully but will still need some instant judgement based on the audience response.

Timing the performances   To keep track of pace and of when significant events occur. A chart made during dress rehearsals and then updated as the plot gathers pace can be a very useful point of reference when harassed actors whisper: 'How long before I go on?' or 'Have I got time to go to the loo?' or an agitated props person confesses: 'I've left the tablecloth at home. Is there still time to run up the road?'

Dealing with emergencies   The stage manager is responsible for 'keeping the show on the road' and the audience oblivious to any hiccups that occur back stage. He or she should try to keep the pantomime rolling along as smoothly as possible when minor problems arise – or, ultimately, call it to a halt if there is a major disaster such as fire. Whether the emergency is major or minor, keeping everybody calm is vital – front- and backstage – and much depends on the stage manager's organisational ability and manner.

Marking the stage   To help the props and scene changes to run smoothly and to make sure everything is consistent and in the right place, the stage floor needs to be marked with slashes of carpet tape, like stamp corners, to indicate the positions and angles at which major items should be placed.

To achieve all this, the stage manager should be very well organised and set up a prompt copy with all the notes required between the relevant pages of the script. To gather all this information together, the following will be needed:

cast list – names (and understudies if used), telephone numbers
staff list – names and telephone numbers of the backstage team and anyone else who might step into the breach
other useful names and telephone numbers (such as caterers, hall organisers, caretakers)
scenes list (details of scenes, characters involved, and any special requirements such as quick costume changes)
properties list
lighting plot
costume plot
prompt copy
sound and special effects plot
plans of the stage and positions of major items

The stage manager's overall aim is to achieve a consistent, professional, technically sound, smooth-running, disciplined and happy production.

Stage hands

Height and strength can be useful, especially if large flats need to be moved, but the main assets are being able to move things calmly, quickly and quietly and being aware of exactly when these moves are needed.

Acting members are sometimes drilled into fulfilling this function, but this can create problems. Actors are likely to be distracted, forget or get into a tizzy if a costume change or an entrance is imminent. It is better to have a separate team who can concentrate properly on the job in hand.

Stage hands sometimes have to appear in front of the audience, in which case they are best either dressed simply in inconspicuous black or appropriately to the play – as lackeys or servants or in national costume, whatever suits the theme, so long as the treatment is consistent.

Wardrobe

I am going to refer to the person in charge of costume as 'she', although undoubtedly there are some excellent men who also undertake this task.

Most of the wardrobe's responsibilities are dealt with before the performance, when either one person or a whole team of people will have been beavering away to find, alter, hire or create from scratch all the costumes required for the production. None the less, it is still useful if the wardrobe mistress can be in evidence backstage to help with difficult or fast changes and to be ever ready with a needle and cotton for instant repairs. A colourful and exciting range of costumes is an essential ingredient of pantomime and how to achieve this is discussed on pages 129-30. It is an opportunity for an imaginative wardrobe mistress to add a little magic to every show, while ensuring that the budget is not overstretched.

The producer and wardrobe need to get together as early as possible. Basic discussions about characters and style can be informally launched long before the production – maybe even a year ahead, if the play has been selected – so that there is ample opportunity to raid jumble sales, junk shops, friends' turn-outs and other sources of clothes and materials that might be in keeping with the theme. Throughout, the costume mistress needs to work closely with the producer to ensure her ideas are in tune with the style of the overall production and reflect the theme and mood of particular scenes. Once the characters have all been cast, measurements can be taken and then the work can begin in earnest. The costumes should make everyone wearing them feel more confident.

Duties

To measure and clothe the cast.

To ensure everything is ready on time, allowing sufficient margin for dealing with alterations and altercations.

To build up and control a team of helpers to sew – even if only hems. But be tactful; if someone is highly skilled, allow them to help with something more challenging and inspiring.

Fast changes To help – or arrange for help to be available – with any difficult or very fast changes of costume.

To have an emergency kit backstage – scissors, thread, safety pins, velcro. Needles already threaded up can save precious moments when an actor shrieks: "Help! My skirt's split and I'm on in five!"

To arrange for any hiring of costumes – and for the collection and return of these and any borrowed items.

To find any accessories required – such as jewellery, hats, gloves, shoes, fans, handbags.

To keep records of costs involved.

To keep close track of who has what – and when, and make sure everything is gathered in safely at the end of the show.

Costume plot – To make a plot of the play's requirements: the costumes needed, the times of changes, when fast or difficult changes are due, and any other special needs.

Properties

There are three basic kinds of properties: big, little and personal.

Large props – like the Sleeping Beauty's bed or Cinderella's coach – are closely linked to the set design. Accordingly, props personnel need to coordinate with the set designer and to abide by his or her decisions over size, colour and shape. In many cases, the areas of responsibility overlap and it is likely that the set designer will want totally to control the manufacture of such items if, like Jack's beanstalk, they are really an integral part of the overall scene.

In conventional plays, pieces of furniture generally need to be borrowed. Usually there are not too many of these in pantomime, for which any furnishings often have to be oversized, wildly colourful or fantastic in some way. They will probably need to be made specially – the set designer and backstage construction team can often be persuaded to come to the rescue.

So it is likely that in the main, the props people will be dealing with the smaller items. There are vast numbers of things required in a pantomime – everything from strings of sausages to magic beans, fairies' wands and witches' cauldrons, flying carpets, golden eggs, magic lamps, pumpkins and any number of signs exhorting the audience to boo, hiss or 'laugh for goodness sake!'

Small personal props, such as watches, handkerchiefs, notebooks (basically, anything worn or pocketed) will need to be discovered by the props but then, once handed over, become the responsibility of the actor concerned – in *theory*. In practice actors are not always as disciplined and responsible as one would hope and, in all fairness, may be hurtling from one mad change to another in a very overcrowded, confined space. So it is useful if the props crew are prepared for emergencies and can check and double-check everything, personal props included.

Duties

Stocklist Keep and update a stocklist showing the items the society already has. Who wants to make another string of sausages when there are already five in the property cupboard? In addition to this, it can be useful to make a note of potentially useful items spotted in the homes of family, friends and fellow actors;

Lynn has a huge plastic lobster; David has a fruit machine; Julie had a vast inflatable champagne bottle at her wedding; Dennis has an enormous blue-flowered potty; John's bright pink chair might convert well into a throne; Patrick has a stuffed crocodile.

Properties

	In stock	Buy or hire	Who making	Set designer organising	Collect from	Who for or OS / on-stage	Needed by page no. (in script)	Checked and or ready	Cost	Returned
ACT ONE										
Eggs		B				ANN	1			
Honey		B				JANE	1			
Pears		B				GILL	1			
Tarts			ME			SUE	1			
Purses			ME			C+B+J+W	1			
Baskets					JACKIE	A+J+G+S	1			
String or lead for cow					SHEILA	VIV	3			
Tree stump				SD		OS	7			
Magic beans in bag			ME			CHRIS	9			
Table & 2 kitchen chairs					JOHN	OS	13			
Flour		B				OS	13			
Eggs		B				OS	13			
Screws, nails, nuts & bolts	S					RAY	13	√		
Spoons	S					OS	13	√		
Dog's bone			JULIE			OS	13	√		
Mixing bowl					JULIE	OS	13			
Wooden spoon (huge)			ROBIN			RAY	13	√		
ACT TWO										
Workable Beanstalk		H				OS	17			
Watering can					ANN	VIV	17			
Fire irons				SD		OS	21			
Cauldron				SD		OS	21			
Coal scuttle				SD		OS	21			
Giant's slippers			ME			OS	21			
Workable descending Pizza			ROBIN			WING	23			
Giant's hand on pole			JULIE			WING	23			
Box giant crunchie-munchies			ME			WING	23			
Golden eggs			ME			P+WING	23/25			
ACT THREE										
String of sausages	S					PIPPA	26	√		
Hot-water bottles					PETER	RAY	27			
Corset	S					RAY	27			
Money	S					TONY	28	√		
Clouds				SD		OS	28			
Hatchet	S					VIV	30	√		
Beanstalk leaves			VAL			FLY	30			
Wedding invitations			DAVID		BOB	R+B+P+A	31			
Trumpet for fanfare						DEREK	31			
Herald's scroll			DAVID			STEW	34			
Flowers			ME			ALL	36			
Balloons		B				FLY				

A typical property listing which shows what is required by whom and whether a source has yet been located. It also makes a useful record of costs involved – invaluable when planning future productions. The props team will, of course, also need to mark up a copy of the script with all the cues for props.

Panto props list   Make a full property list for each production. The play copy's official list may be inadequate or overambitious – and, anyway, producers always add things of their own. The list should say exactly what is needed, when and by whom.

Gathering everything in   Ask the assembled cast if they have any of the necessary items or materials needed, marking down on the list who volunteers what. You will forget who promised particular items otherwise (and so will those who volunteered them, unless reminded). You will also need to consult the list when returning items after the production.

It is useful, too, to have a column to tick on your list when something is located – and delivered or bought – and to note down after the show when each item is returned to its owner or that it has now been added to the society's stocklist.

Marking property positions and cues   Mark up the play copy so that the requirement and movement of props related to the action on and offstage is clear. Give yourself cues to do everything with a good time margin. For example:

> When Goldilocks (front of curtain) says 'What a dear little wood and what a dear little house I can see at the bottom of the hill!'
> 1. Rescue the magic wand from the Big Bad Wolf as soon as he comes off stage.
> 2. Give the bears walking sticks and hats.
> 3. Check mattress is outside window ready for Goldilocks's fall.
> 4. Put the porridge on the table stage left.
> 5. Make sure Baby Bear's nappies are on the chair.
> 6. Double check that SM has angled armchair to ensure it is clear of curtain line.
> 7. Put newspaper on Daddy Bear's chair.

Properties are laid out in order of use – everything from a magic cake and the dame's hot water bottles to the hen's golden egg.

Taking care of everything Many of the items will have been borrowed and the props crew are responsible for the care of these as well as all the items belonging to the society. It can be difficult in the hurly-burly backstage to control everything, but if items are rescued from actors straight away and put back in the right place, there will be less chance of breakage, loss and panic.

Being prepared All the properties need to be clearly laid out and ready in good time. If there is room, a table for each act with the items presented in the right order will help enormously. The props can be shuffled along in turn if space is at a premium so that just the immediate items are to hand. Organisation is the key to success.

The set designer

Like costumes, the set design is a pre-production activity. From production onwards, the set is really in the hands of the stage manager, and so the set designer can generally relax and watch the show – although, once out front, he or she is likely to see bits that need improving and, if time allows, may be tempted to titivate.

The good set designer is imaginative, sympathetic to the mood and aspirations of the show, able to communicate his or her ideas well with those who are creating the set and ultimately with the audience, and has a good relationship with the producer. Now find an artist who fits the bill *and* can work within a tight budget!

Duties

Understanding the play The designer must first assess the overall play and discuss the themes and concepts with the producer.

Planning and presentation of ideas and structure The next step is to present a general overview of how the sets will look and work, considering the technical aspects as well as aesthetics. A scale model is invaluable for demonstrating and discussing these ideas.

Detailed design To design the individual scenes in detail, not only the major scenes but also thinking through the way the front-of-curtain minor scenes can be made more effective and the overall ambience of the hall when the audience arrives.

The creation To implement or oversee the implementation of the structure and painting of the scenery, making sure that any delegation is carefully structured so that the sets work as a whole.

Coordination To coordinate with all the other members of the backstage team and to consider their needs too. (For example, it is no good designing a piece of scenery that blocks a lighting effect.)

Helping props The designer should control and oversee those properties which in effect constitute part of the scenery. The props team may need the designer's skills and help with the creation of large- and small-scale pieces and it is important to achieve a coordinated effect on the stage.

Wowing the audience Ultimately the scenery should look wonderful and sweep the audience into other worlds, bringing the settings to life and contributing to the illusory world on the stage in an exciting and stimulating way.

Safety The sets must be practical, safe and take into account fire regulations.

Stage planning

Cloths

Curtains, (tabs)

Fixed back cloth

Rolled back cloth

Border

Gauze

Properties

Tables

Chairs

Bench and armchair

Flats

Plain flat

Wide and narrow flats

Door flat

Window

Fireplace

Flat with cut-out

Bay window

Pivot

Pivoting flats

Steps and ramps

UP

UP ramp

Different levels

Rostra

Truck

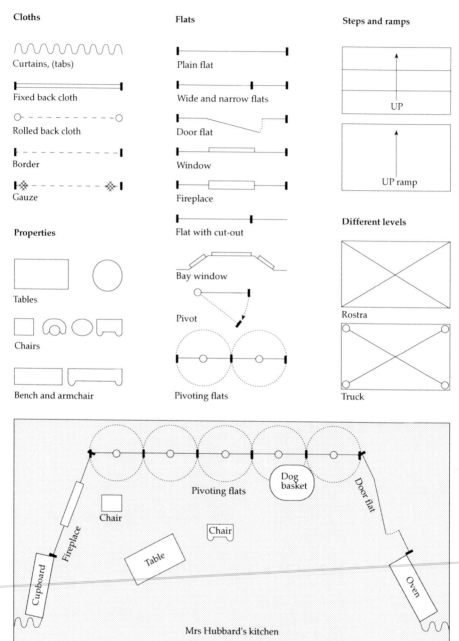

Pivoting flats

Dog basket

Door flat

Chair

Fireplace

Chair

Cupboard

Table

Oven

Mrs Hubbard's kitchen

The producer and the stage designer need to clarify their requirements for each scene very early on so that moves can be planned accordingly. These are the conventional symbols used when planning sets and property location. They can readily be adapted to suit pantomime requirements such as thrones, cauldrons, tree stumps and milestones.

The flats are 'chalked up' ready to be drawn upon and painted.

Lighting

In professional theatre there is a clear distinction between those who design the lighting for plays and those who are responsible for the electric circuits and appliances. In amateur theatre these distinctions blur and it is likely to be a single person (with perhaps, one or two helpers on the mechanical side) who works out the lighting plot, designs the mix of colour and light which will so dramatically affect the presentation, who clambers up ladders and scaffolding to fix lanterns and angle spots and then presses all the buttons and dimmer switches during the performances.

To the uninitiated, this can seem like a world of wizardry and technical jargon. It *is* a very important role and although a complete novice can, with enthusiasm and by mugging it up in library books, manage to light a show adequately, the guidance of someone with experience, combined with little flair, will go a long way. In addition, a clear understanding of electricity and safety is absolutely vital.

Duties

Understanding the play and working well with the team To contribute fully, it is essential that the lighting expert appreciates the nuances of plot and mood in order to do full justice to the production. He or she needs to be involved at the earliest possible time in order to plan ahead properly and work closely with both the producer and the set designer to achieve an integrated whole and a smooth-running lighting plot and execution.

Improving visibility The basic requirement of the lighting is to ensure that the action and players can be clearly seen, so that the audience can better appreciate what is happening on the stage and see everything in greater detail.

Forgive me if this sounds obvious, but it is often forgotten. A whirl of enthusiasm to create special effects and to light particular areas of the stage for dramatic moments (especially when the society does not have a vast range of equipment or power) can result in the emphasis of the lighting for the general scenes being overlooked – so that, for example, if the actors move too far in one direction all their faces plunge into shadow. Plenty of attention must be given to all the stage, with time allowed for fine adjustment to ensure good visibility throughout.

Adding dramatic emphasis   Once good basic lighting has been established so that there are no parts of the stage left in shadow (unless required for some special reason, such as in a dungeon scene), it is time to play with the creative use of colour and light to underline the drama. If this is well done, once again this will help the audience to relate to the plot – for example, the magic look of Aladdin's cave, aglitter with jewels, can be purely a lighting effect.

Time, place and weather   The time of day, from dawn to dusk and dead of night, can be intimated by the appropriate use of light. So can weather – swirling snow or dancing rain, clouds, thunder and lightning.

Moreover, different levels and colours of lighting help to establish whether a scene is taking place outside or inside, in summer or winter, in a hot or cold climate.

Independently of any scenery, lighting effects can also create specific settings such as a gloomy cave, a woodland glade, a boat at sea, the interior of a rich palace, an attic bedroom or a rabbit hole.

Staying in control   Careful planning and remaining calm are important. For the novice, the responsibility can seem quite awesome: the impact on the audience is very powerful if the stage is suddenly plunged into darkness or the house lights refuse to dim or there is a ghastly hushed hiatus when a transformation scene fails to work.

If everything is well organised and thoroughly rehearsed, no such problems will arise, but if some or all of the lighting is hired and does not arrive until the last moment, intensive technical rehearsal may be needed to ensure smooth progress. Never choose a lighting person who is prone to panic!

Sound and special effects

Much of what has been said about sets and lighting applies in a similar way to the sound and special effects personnel. They will need to:

Understand the play.

Plan ahead.

Work well with the team.

Add dramatic emphasis – an explosion, a gunshot, smoke from a dragon's mouth.

Help to establish background factors such as time, place and weather   This can be done, for instance, by a clock chiming the hour or a historical wireless broadcast; the sound of sea and surf, traffic, or fairground music; wind, drumming rain, lightning flashes, fog.

Give the play greater realism   Adding the fine detail to the play, such as doorbells and telephones ringing, horses' hooves, trains arriving, water splashing. These might be taped or mechanical effects.

Stay in control and keep calm.

Contribute flair and fun   Whoever is selected to do lighting and special effects needs to be imaginative and inventive and to have a good sense of humour.

STAND BY
FOR GIANT

JACK Please, I am lost and hungry. Can you give me some food and somewhere to rest?

MRS DREADFUL No! You must run away, and quickly. My husband is a Giant; he eats little boys like you.

JACK But there is a storm brewing out here and I am very hungry. I can help you. Please .... [*He steps inside*]

MRS DREADFUL All right. Perhaps you can make the fires and sharpen the knives and wash the pots.

CUE 7
Rumbles and
footsteps

Suddenly there is a loud rumbling noise and the sound of the Giant's heavy tread. The furniture starts to vibrate.

Thunder
Co-ordinate
with lighting
cues 4 + 5

MRS DREADFUL Here comes the Giant now.

Thunder and lightning add to the drama of his approaching tread. Jack runs towards door.

CUE 9
"Echo-chamber"
microphone

MRS DREADFUL Quickly, hide in this cupboard. *She pushes Jack behind cupboard door as the huge boots of the Giant enter, disappearing above the stage proscenium. He sings:*

Fee-fie-foe-fum - I smell the blood of an Englishman
Oh, be he alive, or be he dead
I'll grind his little bones to make my bread!

Gradually
increase
volume

Fee-fie-foe-fum -Tell the little children they should run
I'm a horrid giant and here I come
Eating little boys is enormous fun

Fee-fie-foe-fum - I am a giant with a rumbling tum
It rolls as loud as a kettle drum
To tell me when it's time to eat someone

Fee-fie-foe-fum - My feet can stamp on everyone
The earth vibrates when I jump and run
Fee-fie-fiddle, fiddle-fie-foe-fum
Fee-fie-fiddle, fiddle-fie-foe-fum

CUE 10
Rusty clanking
chain noise

GIANT Now, where is that little boy I can smell?

Mrs Dreadful turns winding mechanism and a vast giant pizza descends from above.

Lighting, sound and special effects will need to be plotted page by page in the script. Here, each particular sound has been highlighted and 'stand-by' cues shown. The stage manager and property team will also need to mark up a script in this way, while the prompt should highlight pauses and tricky areas. Any changes to the script will need to be updated and clearly indicated.

Make-up

Too often make-up is allocated to anyone who is willing to help, regardless of experience or expertise. Enthusiasm and imagination are more important than experience, for there are oodles of excellent books on the subject. However, in the right hands, make-up can add hugely to the success of the production. Some actors prefer to do their own make-up and can certainly become experts in their own right, but it is still important that there is one person who takes an overall view of the make-up to ensure that the production has a cohesive style and approach. If the cast is large, a team of helpers can work together while the 'expert' concentrates on the more complicated make-up and generally keeps an eye on the rest of the team's efforts.

Duties

Stock control   To look after the make-up stock and buy whatever is required before each production.

Planning ahead   The make-up needs to be well organised. The play should be studied, characters discussed with the producer and individual actors and a plan of campaign for the performances devised, taking into account how much time is required prior to curtain up, who has fast changes and when, and at which points lots of people need help. For example;

> Act 3, Page 43: Six peasants have to mutate into American Indians – need a team to help colour bodies and do face warpaint in ten minutes flat.

Helping define characters   Stage characters in pantomime need to have an instant impact on the audience. Their roles can be exaggerated by the make-up, which can be a lot of fun, especially for such characters as the villains and the dame, animal roles, fairies and witches. A whole range of age groups and degrees of glamour and beauty or ugliness may need to be conveyed.

Instilling confidence in the cast   Good make-up, like the costumes, helps the actors to feel their way into the role and to become somebody quite different from their everyday selves. If the actors are comfortable with the make-up, and excited by the changes they see in the mirror, it will help them enormously to 'get out there and sock it to them'.

Counteracting the draining effect of the lighting   Strong stage lighting can flatten the features and wash out skin colour, so part of the make-up's purpose is to counteract this effect. It is therefore important to establish what lighting will be used when, which colours and how powerful it is going to be.

Wig and hair control   The make-up person is responsible for hairstyles and may need to find, hire or buy, and dress any wigs required, as well as helping with actors' own hairdressing. Whether the make-up person can actually style hair or not varies from one society to another. The make-up person may act merely in an advisory capacity but it is a great bonus if he or she can drum up help or style hair appropriately.

The prompt

A good prompt is a great ally to producer and cast alike. It is not an easy task to fulfil. It requires enormous concentration, with no let-up throughout the performances and no real glory either.

Surprisingly, some people love prompting especially if they enjoy the idea of drama but do not wish to be in the limelight themselves. However, it has to be said that there is little opportunity to join in with the rest of the cast and it is all too easy to end up with a headache because of the intense concentration and poring over small print. This last problem can be alleviated by having a larger duplication of the script and making sure there is a good light in the prompt's corner.

Producers should appreciate the prompt's efforts and help to make their task easier by filling in the prompt with all the necessary background information about the play and players and encouraging early attendance at rehearsals. A prompt who knows the play intimately can be a little more relaxed during the performances.

Even in this role, a sense of humour can be invaluable. In pantomime, the audience will accept and forgive a great deal that would be disastrous in a straight play performance. This is not to say that there is any excuse for a sloppy, disorganised production, but at least in a pantomime if someone does forget a line the prompt who has sufficient confidence can actually get away with walking on to the stage and joining in. The prompt might even be dressed appropriately and be quite visible to the audience, or could walk on with huge notices saying; 'He always forgets this bit' or 'Don't forget to tell them about the treasure!'

Duties

Prompting during the rehearsals   The prompt is an invaluable aid to line-learning and should attend rehearsals at least from the time the first actors put down their scripts – if not before. The prompt can assist the producer greatly by keeping track of the script during rehearsals and marking up cues and practical points so that the producer can concentrate on watching what is happening on the stage.

Prompting during the production   Prompts must be ever ready to come to the rescue when actors lose their lines, so that the show is kept rolling. To do this well, the prompt must have a thorough knowledge of the play, and understand the   individual actors. The prompt needs to be aware of their interpretation, timing and attitude, how sound their line-learning abilities are, and alert to any weak moments when they have regularly had problems in rehearsal.

Being heard and responding quickly   It is pointless for a prompt to whisper so quietly that the actor cannot hear his cue. It is embarrassing for an audience to see an actor struggling to find his words with no sound emerging from the prompt corner. A clear, confident cue is always a welcome relief.

The good prompt, who knows the play and actors intimately, will be aware of problems very quickly and should be able to give the line before the audience have even had a chance to notice that there is a hitch.

Being able to see the stage and the actors' expressions is an enormous help. That nervous mouth twitch may indicate a problem arising and the raised questioning eyebrow or fluttering of hands can be a trigger to the prompt to come in quickly.

Being sensitive   The prompt should be very conscious of the actors' reactions at all times and be aware of their needs. The prompt who jumps in unnecessarily every time an actor pauses for dramatic effect is perhaps almost as irritating as the prompt who lets an actor flounder around ad-libbing furiously and then says; 'But you seemed to be coping so well without me!'

Controlling the flow   If actors suddenly jump ahead or back in the script – perhaps because there is a similar line or cue that almost repeats itself – it is the responsibility of the prompt to guide the actors back into the correct place in the script. If the prompt fails to do this, or the actors do not respond to the prompt's cues and obliviously continue with the momentum of the new position in the play, the prompt, without deserting his or her post, should try to get word to the stage manager that the actors have leaped ahead (or back), since the repercussions can be devastating to others involved. Actors may have to change costumes at lightning speed or change their lines to suit the new circumstances while technicians may need to organise revised sound effects or caterers prepare the interval beverages at breakneck speed, and so on.

Chaos may be reigning backstage at such moments until some degree of normality is restored: at such times it is some comfort to remember that the audience will often be totally unaware that there has been any problem at all!

The prompt copy   In some theatres, the prompt acts as assistant to the stage manager and is responsible not only for prompting the actors but also for prompting the lighting, sound, special effects and so on. In any case, the prompt should make up a 'prompt copy', taking into account the headache factor already mentioned. Divide up the script into a folder and insert loose leaves in between. Allow lots of space for notes on all the cues, front- and backstage, and for marking in actors' dramatic pauses and potential stumbling points.

Make sure the file and paper used are sturdy enough to take the continuous handling throughout rehearsals and performances – thin, punched paper will tear all too quickly. Ensure too that you do not underestimate the amount of information it will need to contain. Make sure there is room to accommodate all the rehearsal notes, the backstage cues, and the last-minute changes that are bound to occur. This document will be an invaluable point of reference for the producer during rehearsals and, later, for the stage manager in performances; he may well use it as the basis for his backstage management.

Front of house

The front-of-house personnel are the first people that the audience meet when they arrive so it is fundamental that they are:

    cheerful
    charming
    diplomatic
    unflustered
    smiling
    able to cope with emergencies
    able to handle money responsibly.

Duties

The amount of responsibility placed upon the front of house varies from merely selling tickets and programmes on the door to advance ticket sales and tidying up the hall at the end of the run. Depending on the range of duties, they are undertaken by a team or by one person with occasional help. The following factors need to be covered:

Sale of tickets   In house and in advance, and the collection and accounting of any monies received.

The venue   To ensure the venue is prepared beforehand – seating and table arrangements, numbering seats, entrances, photographs, flowers, tablecloths, music playing.

Catering   Ensuring that the preparation of any food and drink is undertaken on time and organising waiters and waitresses, if required.

A warm welcome   Greeting everyone who arrives and making them feel good the minute they arrive.

Ushers and programme selling   Lots of smiling people to help the audience find their places and relax.

The raffle   If a raffle is required, front of house will need to organise the collection of gifts, sale of raffle tickets, draw and presentation of prizes.

Reservations   Dealing with tickets held at the door and any reserved places.

Keeping in touch with backstage   The front of house may need to communicate with the stage manager; for example, to indicate whether the play should begin now or whether curtain up should be held back for five minutes because there is a last-minute rush of arrivals at the door.

Latecomers   Dealing with latecomers quietly and efficiently.

Saying goodbye   Seeing everyone out with a smile at the end of the show and storing up any congratulations to be passed on appropriately.

Safety   It is ultimately the front-of-house responsibility to ensure exits are kept clear in case of fire and that the seating arrangements are in keeping with safety rules.

In general, the front of house is responsible for the audience. Much depends on the organisation and site of the venue. There may be a bar to staff, a cloakroom for coats, somebody may need to ensure that the loo paper does not run out and that the snow is swept off from the entrance and that old ladies and gentlemen are helped up the steep steps.

It is really a case of thinking ahead, imagining how the audience will be feeling as they arrive and working out how best to help them to relax and enjoy a truly happy evening with you all. For that, ultimately, is what the society as a whole, front- and backstage, is striving towards.

5

Rehearsals: mob control

It is always best to avoid sweeping statements because there are so many exceptions just waiting to undermine a bland comment. However, it has certainly been the case in my experience of amateur theatre that most of the producers and directors have already been 'the boss' in some other walk of life and so can take directing in their stride. A good number have been schoolteachers with a sprinkling of lecturers and managers well used to controlling teams of people. There have also been producers who have risen through the ranks, having been involved in staging shows for years, thereby gaining considerable respect and authority. Some are former professionals. Some are there simply because they have faith in a particular script and want to see it through, one way or another. Others are persuaded into the position because no one else will do the job. A few find themselves in the role of producer because they had too many drinks at the party after the last production and admitted in a wild moment that they fancied 'having a go'.

By whatever route they may have arrived at the helm, the producer and/or director are in charge now and the success of the pantomime will largely depend on their dedication and enthusiasm. So, what is the best way to begin?

The first rehearsal

It is good to start with the full team gathered, front- and backstage, so that everyone can find out about the play and meet all the other people who are going to be involved. It will a social event, not just a rehearsal, and this is of value because part of the fun of amateur dramatics is meeting everyone, catching up on news and forming friendships.

The first rehearsal is an important evening because it will establish in everyone's minds what is expected of them, what kind of production this will be and whether the experience is going to be enjoyable and worthwhile. Will it justify giving up heaven knows how many cosy evenings at home?

The pep talk

With everybody gathered, this is prime opportunity for the producer to talk about the production, the approach, the aims, the timing, and whatever is most pertinent. It is the moment to fire enthusiasm, to get the teams gelling and to set up goals. A good, lively pep talk to the general gathering should be followed by individual chats with particular people. Try to make everyone feel special and important, no matter how small they might believe their contribution to be.

Be positive, happy and purposeful. If at the end of this first meeting, you can send everyone away excited about the production, pleased and proud to be involved, clear about the aims and their particular responsibilities and confident that this will be a brilliant show, you will have achieved a great deal.

Understanding the play as a whole

Some companies choose this first rehearsal as an opportunity to read through the whole script for the first time with everyone in their roles. This helps to create an overall view of the play and the relationships between different actors. Whether you do this will depend on the time available and on how often the play has been read as a whole during auditions. There is little point in having yet another read-through if you have already had three or four with everyone there.

If you have only ever picked out smaller sections as audition pieces, it is absolutely vital that the cast and backstage team have a complete view of the play. This may have to be a slightly edited version, omitting (but giving a résumé of) areas dependent on technical wizardry, slapstick and anything else highly visual. The main thing is to make sure the entire plot is understood by everyone before it is segmented up for the rehearsals that will follow.

It can be all too easy for lighting, props and costume, for example, to say, 'I'll come along when you have a full run.' and so delay getting their tasks under way. If they were not at the auditions, grab them for this first rehearsal if you possibly can.

Music

This can be a good time to make a first attack on the music, with everyone there to join in. A cheery sing-along to the piano will be good fun and provide a very useful grounding. Music will be a vital element of a pantomime and needs to be a priority from the beginning. You will, of course, need to have primed the pianist first and given him or her a chance to become familiar with the score.

Paperwork

At this launch rehearsal, you will be giving out scripts, rehearsal schedules, telephone trees, music and so on. Lucky producers have the luxury of an assistant, perhaps someone who wants to gain production experience, but whether it is a solo or a joint responsibility, somebody must ensure that everyone has what is needed and that a clear record is kept of who has received what. And tell everyone to write their names on their scripts straight away because some people always lose them.

Set up a register. Have a diary of the rehearsal dates with plenty of room to write down comments. There will always be people bouncing up to apologise in advance: 'I can't make Thursday 17th or Tuesday week because. . . ' They frequently choose to impart this information while you are watching a particularly difficult scene in action, whispering in your ear while you are in the middle of making notes about moves, watching the stage and sifting twenty-odd things around in your brain at once. So have a register and write it all down – or ask them to fill it in. Otherwise you will simply forget and when the night in question arrives you will be cursing their nonarrival, keeping others waiting for them and ending up with an unnecessarily disorganised evening. When you later accuse the actor of not turning up, you will be informed 'But I told you *ages* ago that I was away in Brighton then.'

ABSENTEES (LET'S HAVE THE GOOD EXCUSES THEN!)

JANUARY

Saturday 7	JOHN IN GERMANY
Sunday 8	
Monday 9	
Friday 13	SUSAN leaving early (8.45) DAVID AWAY
Sunday 15	
Monday 16	
Thursday 19	
Friday 20	
Sunday 22	CHRIS AWAY
Monday 23	ON COURSE
Thursday 26	
Friday 27	
Sunday 29	
Monday 30	Sorry Gill - can't make it till 9 PM love

FEBRUARY

Thursday 2	
Friday 3	
Sunday 5 RUN THROUGH	PIANIST LATE (Sue will 'stand in')
Monday 6	
Wednesday 7	
Friday 10	
Sunday 12 DRESS REHEARSAL	
Monday 13	PROMPT UNAVAILABLE - Find someone else!
Thursday 16 RUN THROUGH	
Friday 17	
Saturday 18 Technical rehearsal	
Sunday 19 DRESS REHEARSAL	
Monday 20 DRESS REHEARSAL	

Absentee form: hopefully, this will remain blissfully empty - but generally there are going to be a few clashes of commitment and the producer needs to know when these will occur so that he or she can plan accordingly.

Of course, it is to be hoped that there will not be too much absenteeism. Part of the pep talk will be to impress upon the cast how vital it is to attend *all* the rehearsals, for the sake of everyone else concerned. But there are other factors in people's lives and occasional clashes are bound to occur. Get it all in writing so that you are aware right from the start of the predictable nonarrivals, late arrivals and early disappearances. Then you will be able to plan accordingly. Stress from rehearsal one that communication is important and make sure that everyone has your telephone number and can at least let you know if something unpredictable happens.

Blocking moves

Having set the ball rolling and fired enthusiasm all round, the next step is to plot and practise all the moves. To some extent this has to be a trial-and-error process. No matter how much thinking you have done at home, things always look different 'in the flesh'. None the less, the thought processes at the planning-at-home stage will have helped to establish at least the basic logic of the moves.

At this stage, the actors will still be clutching their scripts, which limits their gestures and arm movements, but this does not matter as long as you are concentrating on entrances and exits, the ebb and flow across and around the stage and the positions where people will stop, stand, sit, lean, turn and pause. Some of these moves will change and mutate with later interpretation and characterisation, but this pattern of movement is the blueprint upon which you will build the structure of the pantomime.

In the early stages of rehearsal, scripts will still be very much in evidence and will be needed, not only for lines, but also for marking down moves.

Being organised

Make sure everyone brings along a pencil and a rubber – take a few spares yourself for those who always forget. As the actors go through the motions, they should write down the moves in the margins of the scripts. There are bound to be some changes so it is preferable not to let anybody loose on the script with a pen. If the play copies are borrowed or hired, then it is even more important that they are not permanently marked or damaged in any way. Any pencil marks on borrowed scripts will need to be removed before the play copies are returned.

It can be useful to bring with you some miniature plans of the stage to draw in the more complicated moves for your own records and to mark down positions of individuals in crowd scenes. This will be much quicker than writing down reams of words and will be easier to understand afterwards.

If possible, take apart your own version of the script and put it in a file with these stage plans and useful space for notes opposite each page of the script so you can see everything at a glance.

If you have not already done so at audition stage, make a note of everybody's height. Put them in your register, if you like. This will be invaluable when grouping large numbers of people or pairing up for musical sequences.

Stage terminology

Make sure that any newcomers are familiar with stage terminology. It can be very unnerving for a beginners suddenly to find themselves in the midst of all this jargon, not understanding any of the directions they are being given.

Provide stage plans with the terms and positions clearly shown to those who need help in interpreting where you are telling them to go. They will soon be as familiar as everyone else with upstage, downstage, tabs and aprons, but a little homework will speed up the learning process.

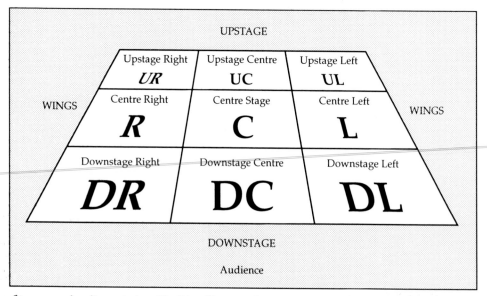

Stage areas: handing out plans like this will ensure that newcomers quickly grasp the terminology.

Things to avoid

The traffic jam This occurs when too many people try to move through an exit or entrance at any one time. Spread your forces. Alternate sides and approaches.

The crash A frequent hazard, especially after a heavy night's rehearsal, when jaded actors move towards each other from opposite directions and collide, whether at an exit or entrance or while on stage. Ensure there is plenty of room to move and choreograph the whole manoeuvre properly. Otherwise you may find two actors diving from side to side, desperately trying to avoid each other, or discover there is a rhinoceros in your midst who charges on regardless.

Illogical moves Remember what is supposed to be where offstage, so that suitable exits and entrances are used. If it is a woodland scene, there may be a wide choice of exits, but an actor who has come in from the front door and is going back into the street needs to go out the same way. Ensure all the actors are aware of the 'geography' of the world represented beyond the visible stage.

Walking through the fittings Furniture, walls and scenery are highly unlikely to be in place at the earliest rehearsals so use whatever is at hand to create substitutes – establish the necessary barriers, places to sit and entrances to pass through. Usually a variety of chair formations on the stage can represent all manner of things from sofas to front doors, fireplaces, arched palace gates, Cinderella's coach, Jack's beanstalk or Snow White's coffin. Chalk can also be used to indicate distinct areas but can all too easily be overlooked and walked across.

Forgetting to use the whole stage This is a common problem when rehearsals take place at another venue or if the stage extension is not built until the last week. Rehearsals have a way of ingraining information into the actors' brains and if they have always moved in a particular manner it will soon become semi-automatic and hard to override later. The line-learning becomes part of the process too – moves often trigger lines, and vice versa. Remember to take into account all the different areas that are available right from the beginning. By the same token, do not *over*estimate the space available if the stage is smaller than the rehearsal room.

Even when the rehearsal stage is the one for the performances, some actors tend to hang about at the back or hog the front. Make sure there is a good variety of movement and that all the stage is used appropriately.

Upstaging Some actors delight in stealing the scene intentionally but upstaging can be an unconscious act or result from bad direction. Make sure the position of one actor does not force another to have to turn upstage. If this is for some reason, inevitable or desirable, do not prolong the situation, and do ensure that the upstaged actor increases volume to compensate.

Moves that look uncomfortable Too much crossing of actors on the stage looks awkward, especially if one of them is speaking at the time.

Hesitant moves and short bobbing about will look nervous and alien. Make sure actors move with a purpose.

Using the wrong arm will hide the body and look clumsy: always use the upstage arm so that the body is not covered.

Make sure actors are kept clear of entrances and exits about to be used. If the Ugly Sisters have to make a grand sweeping entrance, giggling, arm in arm, with their crinolines all about them – or storm off the stage in a huff – they will not appreciate having to clamber over Buttons and Cinderella barring their way. Train the actors to anticipate everybody's entrances and exits – not just their own.

Turning inward does not look as good as turning outward. Often you will see novice actors spinning around like tops trying to feel for the correct way to turn. The trick is to turn 'through' the audience, facing them first and then following with the body. Once actors get into the swing of it, turning the right way becomes natural.

Making the moves look good

The moves are, in part, a mechanical process, shifting the actors about the stage to keep entrances clear for those about to enter or leave and to allow all the moves to flow smoothly without blocking, congestion or collision. But they have aesthetic and dramatic value too.

Carefully planned groupings please the eye and, in a way, the good producer 'paints pictures' on the stage, using the actors as the medium. This is an element that is often considered closely when creating a musical number but it is important throughout a production. Always try to make groups look interesting and balanced, and to reflect the situation being enacted.

Stand at the back, half-close your eyes – no, don't go to sleep! Take another look at the pattern the actors are making on the stage. Does it appear to strike the right balance? Does it seem attractive, interesting? Does it convey the feeling of what is happening? Is the right person dominant?

More concentrated rehearsal

Having blocked in the basic moves, the next stage of rehearsals should concentrate on individual sections of play, working with smaller groups of people in greater concentration. Having painted the outline, now you begin to fill in the details.

While the producer still keeps an eye on the overall pattern on the stage, he or she will also be helping individual actors to establish their characters and discover their relationships with the rest of the team on the stage. Dramatic techniques are discussed in more detail in Chapter Six but this is the time when voice, movement, humour and interpretation can be explored, tested, decided and improved.

In many ways this is one of the most interesting stages of rehearsal, before the pressures of the impending deadline and the distractions and interruptions that become inevitable once all the other aspects such as lighting, properties, scene changes and costume are all vying for attention. Make the most of the time before these interruptions arise. The rehearsals need a solid foundation now to be able to continue successfully through those final weeks.

Stop and go

When you feel something is wrong, correct it there and then; try the scene once more, make any adjustments and then run it again. This constant repetition not only helps to improve the particular scene, honing it to perfection, it will also help the actors to remember their moves and lines.

Line learning

Once the moves are basically plotted and familiar, get the lines learned as soon as possible. It is so much easier to act when the scripts are not being clutched like a lifeline, obscuring the face and hampering moves.

When the books are first relinquished, the actors tend to slide back into less polished performances while they flounder around, groping for their lines, feeling exposed without the protection of the script to hang on to. 'I knew them all at home,' they protest. 'I was word perfect in the bath.' It does feel different up on the stage and can be nerve-racking the first time. So the sooner this obstacle is behind you all, the better. And a good solid chunk of rehearsal time without scripts will give the actors much more confidence when facing their first real audience.

Remember that it is also very important to absorb the sense of the lines, the meaning and the logic, the reasons behind them and how they are carrying the plot forward. Then, if the actual lines desert the memory, some sensible replacement can be found.

Sometimes, if the actors have learned their lines really well – but only by rote – they become so automatic that the actor is almost unaware of what he is saying. It can be a terrifying sensation for the actor when he suddenly comes to on stage and has no idea where he is in the script. He has been speaking without thinking and is totally lost. It takes a lot of concentration to be aware all the time of the flow of the plot as well as everything else, but it is important.

If any actors have particular problems learning lines, encourage and advise. Give them moves that create a link and a stimulus. Suggest that they might tape-record the scenes involved, perhaps with someone else reading the other parts. This recording can be played over and over – in the car, while cooking the evening meal or whatever. *Hearing* the lines is important. You don't really listen to your own lines unless you tape them, and this does help: not only will it aid learning but hearing how it sounds will help you to improve delivery, too.

Learning the lines in conjunction with the cues is vital. They are intrinsically linked, with the cue (like some moves) the automatic trigger for the words that are to come.

Go over difficult patches where the lines break down repeatedly.

Make the most of rehearsal time

While one scene is being rehearsed on stage, actors not involved can get together somewhere else (preferably in another room, if one is available) and thrash through areas that need extra practice to establish difficult lines or complicated moves. This is good use of the limited time available and is, anyway, less boring for the actors than watching the same scene several times over. There is nothing more frustrating than thinking, Ah – at last! My bit is coming up now, and waiting ready in the wings, relieved to be doing something at last – only to hear the producer say 'Right! let's try that scene again, folks.' However right and necessary the repetition, it can become tedious for those not involved. Keep everybody busy and working hard and you will have a happier team and a better end result.

Joint exploration and discovery

Producers should resist the temptation to tell the actors exactly how to act each line and interpret every nuance of character. Encourage them to find their own way into the part. Never demand (as do many producers, leaping up on the stage every other minute or so) that they *must* say it *this way*, holding their arms *so*, and walking *thus*. Such a play will end up full of robots feeling that, unless they parrot the producer's interpretation, they are failing somehow. Avoid limiting them and work together through the possibilities. Do not close any doors yet. There may be any number of ways to achieve the best performance.

DOOR

U.R. ◄

ADDRESS ◄
AUDIENCE

ENTERS ◄
U.R.

CLAB HANDS ◄
IN JOY - MOVES
TO JACK; TAKES
HIM D.L.

HOLD SILENCE
COUNT TO 6

SITS ON
CHAIR

✱ N·B
Tell Props
need handky with
wet sponge inside for
squeezing out tears.

MRS HUBBARD   No, Woof! Woof! Honestly, ever since I put the cat flap in the door and fed him on Whiskas, he hasn't been the same. Nice dog. Sit! there you are, now I'll fetch you a bone. Oh, I forgot, there are none left. Not unless Jack has bought some at the market when he sold the cow.

Voice heard off:

JACK   Mother! Mother, I am home. It has been a wonderful day. Let me in so I can show you what I have.

MRS HUBBARD   That's my boy. He sounds happy – he must have sold Buttercup after all. [*She opens the door*] Well, Jack, my lovely boy, what have you got for me?

JACK   Oh, mother, I met the Princess – and a French runner bean man and I sold Buttercup – and -

MRS HUBBARD   You've sold Buttercup! At last! That is marvellous news! Where is the money then? You haven't spent it all, Jack, have you?

JACK   No, Mother. It isn't money the Runner-bean man gave me for Buttercup. It is something special, something magic – Look, he gave me these. [*He pours the beans out on to the table.*]

MRS HUBBARD   [*staring in silence for a moment*] This is what he gave you, Jack? This is all you have in exchange for Buttercup, for a whole big cow?

JACK   Yes, Mother. But listen, they are magic beans. The man said they will make my fortune and then I can marry the princess. Why, Mother, whatever is the matter?

Mrs Hubbard starts to ✱ *howl. Toby joins in.*

MRS HUBBARD   Oh, Jack, how could you! Buttercup was our only hope. Now we have nothing left. What use are these useless magic beans, you foolish stupid boy? We shall starve now – starve, I tell you, starve – BOO HOO!

↖ DOG-HOWL IN
UNISON EVEN
LOUDER.

The producer's script will soon become littered with scribbled instructions and alterations. These notes will form the core of production information for all the team, in particular the stage manager's or prompt copy and will be referred to constantly during succeeding rehearsals.

As she boohoos, the sound of a moo-mooo is heard outside, joining in.

OPEN 'COW FLAP' TO show cow's head!

RISING!

JACK   *[going to door]* It is Buttercup! She must have run away. *[He lets her in]* Buttercup, you naughty girl. What are you doing here?

MRS HUBBARD   That cow's as daft as you are. Now your precious runner bean man will probably sue us into the bargain, or take us to prison for stealing her back. Oh Jack – you and your fine notions of marrying a Princess. See where they have got us. We shall starve and be thrown into prison. These useless beans can go straight out into the compost heap. *[She scoops up the beans and throws them into the audience.]* There! That's got rid of them.

N.B. TELL PIANIST CAST NEEDING 2-3 lines of music to get into line!

SONG: *'We're going to starve'*

We're going to starve and go to prison
Boo-hoo! It really is a crime
There's no solution
But facing retribution
We'll have to serve some penal time

ALL MARCH IN LINE to D.R.

Mrs Hubbard SOLO

The cow's run away from 'Arry Coe
And those magic beans will never grow.
We've got no money
It's not very funny
Jack has sold us down the line

MARCH L

Were getting thinner (so much thinner)
We live on air-air-air-air-air
What is for dinner?
A slice of nothing there - there's nothing there

FACE FRONT
ARMS OUT
HOLD TUMS

ALL

We're going to starve and go to prison
Boo hoo! We sob and scream and wail
No eggs or cream
We don't have a bean
They're bound to cart us off,
Bound to cart us off,
Bound to cart us off to jail

SEPARATE + MARCH IN OPPOSITE DIRECTIONS
MARCH BACKWARDS AND COLLIDE →!←
RECOVER FROM COLLISION + REFORM INTO SINGLE LINE

Exeunt singing
They're bound to cart us off,
Bound to cart us off,
Bound to cart us off to jail

DOWN STEPS + EXIT THROUGH AUDIENCE, STILL SINGING.

Personal relations

The success of all the rehearsals, and of the performances largely depends on maintaining a happy but hard-working crew of people, all striving towards creating a lively and effective production. To attain this end, the producer needs to be attuned to several potential problem areas.

Discipline

Sounds a bit like school, but then, as I remarked earlier, lots of producers are teachers – or should have been. And, by default, every producer becomes one for the duration of the production, guiding the rest of the actors through a creative enterprise. Try to avoid using phrases and expletives like these – or worse!

'Shut up! Shut up!'
'Get on stage *now*, please!'
'What time do you call this?'
'Witches, it's your cue. Where the hell are you, Witches?''
Will you please shut up! You're making so much noise down here, I can't hear the folks on stage.'
'Will somebody please strangle that child!'
'Jacky, get *off* the stage, will you? I really can't have you up there measuring inside legs while the scene's running.
'I don't know who that is talking in the wings but you are behaving thoroughly selfishly. Go *away!*'
'I simply *will no*t tolerate such sloppy attitudes!'

If the cast are well disciplined and unselfish, and the rehearsals are well planned and organised, the producer can hope not to need to raise his or her voice too often in this manner. Although the social aspects and fun and laughter are vital and positive elements, there is a time and place for these and when rehearsals are under way, too much chatter can be very annoying. The players cannot rehearse if noise levels build up, so it is essential to insist on quiet.

Neither can actors rehearse properly with too many missing bodies and so turning up, and turning up on time is also important. The players will need to be self-disciplined, to be aware of their responsibilities to the play as a whole, to think ahead and be constructive. If the producer is all these things, then the cast and backstage crew may follow a good example. But it doesn't always happen!

Timing and Pace

Throughout rehearsals, the cast will need to be encouraged to speed up entrances and cues, to keep the pace flowing. Often it takes repeated reminders or the cast will slip back into a less concentrated attack. All the timing and pauses will need to be carefully structured, rehearsed and 'nagged about'.

One disgruntled or disruptive element can upset the whole balance. There is, however, often a good reason for grievances or bad temper and the good producer is sensitive to undercurrents and feelings as well as the obvious activity on stage.

Unfortunate personality clashes

There will always be some people who do not hit it off or have strongly opposed attitudes. If you already are aware of this, prior to the casting, it can be borne in mind, but there are limits to what you can do and how much anyone should bend to avoid such problems. The best answer is just to be aware of the situation and try to avoid inflaming it in any way.

Private problems

If someone is having problems at home, with the family or at work, with financial difficulties or health worries, then extra stress of any kind will make them more touchy during rehearsals.

Amateur dramatics is often an escape from such problems: pretending to be somebody else is very therapeutic, of course, and the fun and total commitment of rehearsals is wonderful for taking the mind off problems. It is, along with sport, one of the ways in which grown-ups revert to the play of childhood, and it makes us feel good.

The downside is that rehearsals take up much time and energy, and if someone's marriage is rocky, for instance, being out too much can lead to jealousy and anger. So when the producers ask for an extra rehearsal the next night, they may unwittingly be lighting the blue touch paper.

And if two people whose marriages are foundering happen to be cast opposite each other as romantic leads, they may get carried away. Drama groups are notorious for love affairs. Michael Green in his *The Art of Coarse Acting* suggests that the worst love match for the production as a whole is when the stage manager and the prompt have a secret fling. Heaven help those on stage waiting for a cue or the curtains to close!

The producer cannot pry into everybody's private lives but needs to be aware that whenever numbers of people gather together to work closely, there will be other factors affecting attitudes as well as those immediate to the play.

Lessen the aggravation of such problems by being organised, not overtiring the cast, keeping everybody informed so that, for instance, there is no time wasted and fury aroused by people turning up to a rehearsal that has been cancelled. And above all, remain sensitive to the possibility of these emotional factors. The big plus of all this hard work and interaction is that the close-knit team can become almost like family and many long-lasting friendships are formed through amateur dramatics.

Constructive, not destructive criticism

Guidance is a good thing. Damning comments, rudeness, sarcasm and impatience can only be destructive. Acting is all about confidence and this often has to be built up slowly. A casual hurtful comment can be very damaging. *Help* people to improve.

You want, of course, to attain the best possible production and this may mean quite a lot of criticism of what is happening up on stage, but do not be brutal. A quiet chat about interpretation in the pub afterwards may, ultimately, achieve far more that a sarcastic public put-down. Reserve your brutality for the masses when discipline breaks down.

Keep the enthusiasm going

This can be very hard in the middle stage of rehearsals. When everyone sets out, there is an initial flush of enthusiasm, which tends to peter out when the real hard slog sets in. Then, at the end, when the costumes arrive and the sets appear, these give a whole new impetus to the production: the excitement – and fear – of the approaching real audience and the coming-together of all the elements boost the energy levels back up again.

But midway rehearsals often hit the doldrums.

The best way to keep enthusiasm alive is to remain enthusiastic and positive yourself. Remind everyone of the impending deadline that so they do not become complacent. Keep building on what you have, constantly improving, not just repeating. Change things if it will make them better – do not be too lazy to do so or browbeaten by possible backstage demands or grumbling actors. Have the courage of your convictions. If there is constant stimulation and a sense of moving forward all the time, the cast will be less likely to become dulled by the inevitable going-over of particular scenes.

Don't be boring or bored yourself or you will end up with a boring play. Keep the bubbles rising. And keep the laughter flowing.

Do not fall into the trap of working mainly on the good bits and the best actors – this can be a temptation because they are the most satisfactory to see and mould. Make sure *all* the sections are given their due time and commitment. *Be fair.*

One of the advantages of rehearsing in small groups and then running acts later rather than earlier is that there is something new for everyone to see when they eventually watch what the others have been up to in their absence. Moreover, the others then have the benefit of an audience reaction from the rest of the mob, who see their sections of the play fresh and for the first time.

Special or extra rehearsals

Throughout the early stage of rehearsals, other specialised parts of the play which require concentrated attention – such as music and choreography – will have been dealt with, often in specific rehearsals dedicated to these aspects. There may also be rehearsals for children, organised independently of the adult rehearsals. These are dealt with in detail in Chapters Seven and Ten respectively.

The main thing to remember is that every production has different requirements and inevitably certain sections will need extra attention – fights, slapstick scenes, complicated crowd scenes and those with special effects. Scenes with only two or three actors may be allocated special time so as not to keep other people waiting around unnecessarily.

When such things can be anticipated, the rehearsal schedule should be planned right from the beginning to include them but you may still need some additional rehearsals to cover sticky bits or areas that are obviously proving more demanding than expected or to help a new actor step into the breach if someone else has to drop out.

Line rehearsals may also be called when the actors just sit in a circle and hammer out the lines fast and furiously, to help get the script 'under their belts', to speed up delivery and reaction to cues. All this helps to establish vital extra pace once the cast are back on the stage again.

Run-throughs

When all the preparatory work has been done, the moves are plotted, the characters well on the way and lines beginning to flow, it will be time to run the acts as a whole and then, later on, to do one or two complete run-throughs of the whole pantomime.

This helps to establish continuity, to assess the overall flow and feel of the play and to check if there are any practical problems, as when someone screams in anguish: 'I can't do it. I can't be in this song now because you've already asked me to take over Julian's part and I'll be changing into the frog's costume.' Or: 'You're joking! There's no way I can imply that I'm whispering the secret to her now because she's just proved in the last scene that she already knows all about it.' Or: 'Sorry, Gill, but we can't have the table there any more because Terry says that's the only area where he can possibly light the transformation scene.'

Running whole acts and scenes helps all the people concerned, back- and front stage, to understand the general timing and to be ready in plenty of time for their entrances and cues. None the less, the producer will still be interrupting as necessary until all the sections of the play are really flowing well.

Properties and prompt

The support staff certainly need to be in evidence as early as possible. However, there is little point in the props people panicking to get all the hand-held objects ready while the actors are still clutching scripts and so cannot cope with holding cups and saucers, swords, trumpets or whatever. But someone will need to round up and set the stage furniture right from the beginning, and as soon as the books are dropped, the props people really do need to be there in person, ready to hand out suitable objects – if not the actual ones, substitutes with which to practise.

Many a local hall's crockery is raided on these occasions, but it is better to use the society's own things than risk bad feeling by breaking or losing some other group's china or glass.

A good prompt knows the play thoroughly and comes along as soon as possible – not necessarily at the first rehearsal but as soon as the first actor puts his or her book down. Otherwise producers will find that they have their noses glued to the script, prompting instead of watching the moves.

Dress rehearsals

Always have at least one dress rehearsal fairly early on – perhaps as early as three weeks before the first performance. This has the advantage of cutting through complacency and panicking the costume department into action. Many of the costumes will not be ready and, obviously, the hired ones will not have arrived, but it still helps to establish where the gaps lie and whether extra sewing help needs to be drafted in.

Long dresses should be worn early on, even if not the actual garments, for they change the actor's movement quite dramatically. The dame will certainly need practice, especially if this is the first time he has worn a gown and high-heeled shoes!

A dress rehearsal one week before should include as much of the scenery changes as practicable, all the props (except perhaps hired ones), all the lighting and special

In an ideal world, all the costumes will be ready for the first dress rehearsal — but often the world is far from ideal.

effects available at that time and definitely all the make-up. The one week that remains will be invaluable in sorting out any omissions and hitches and making adjustments as required.

Fast changes of costume and/or make-up need a good deal of practice to run smoothly and a team of helpers may be needed to assist those actors faced with such challenges as having to leap out of a full witch-doctor's outfit and headdress and wriggle into a mermaid's body, wig and tail. The more rehearsal, the better. At this stage, it is still possible to write in a little extra dialogue, a song, an audience game or some such filler if the change proves totally out of the question in the time available.

It is quite helpful to have these first, very complicated and time-consuming dress rehearsals on, say, a Sunday afternoon, rather than an evening when there is only ever three hours at most and there is pressure to vacate the hall before closing time (the hall's and the pub's!). An evening is never long enough, especially since the first hour is spent trying on clothes and generally fussing!

Give the cast and crew plenty of warning that this is going to be a long rehearsal and tell them to bring along a few sandwiches and beverages so that the rehearsal will not be broken up by the demands of rumbling stomachs and fretful families back home. Children may well come and watch, so that baby-sitting is not a problem – but, if this is the case, do see if someone can be allocated to be in charge of them so that they do not disrupt proceedings.

Good beginnings and ends

Throughout rehearsals it is vital to ensure that the two ends of the evening's entertainment are given special attention – that the show has a superb beginning and an even better finale. You may hope that the middle will be pretty good as well,

The photographer from the local press often arrives just in time to interrupt a vital point in the dress rehearsal.

but a great start gives the audience confidence and a smashing end is something they will carry away with them as their final memory of the performance. So the two extreme ends do matter a great deal.

Rehearse the line-up lots of times, too. If it is given only scant attention just when everyone thinks they have finished, it will always look like an afterthought and let down the whole show. And if you wish to have encores, practise those as well.

Maintaining the magic

Do let the audience believe in you and the world you are creating, on and off stage. Try to keep in character right until you are completely out of sight and sound.

Keep clear of sight lines. Do not let the audience see you half on, hovering, or bits of your body poking out.

Be quiet, especially in the wings or near the stage. It is surprising how far sound travels.

If something goes wrong, keep the play flowing. Never say, 'Sorry!'

Smile, smile, smile! This is especially important for chorus work. Don't let concentration or nerves kill the happy faces. Beam out and make the audience feel welcome.

Keep the pace flowing. During rehearsals, good solid practice will have improved and perfected the pace of the play, but remind the cast of its importance now. They must be fast on line cues, and on entrances, entering *almost* before they are needed. The stage must never be left empty, waiting for an entrance, or with actors making up conversation until another one appears.

Ride the laughter. Remind the cast that the audience will be a new element and will affect the performance in many ways, not least of which is laughter. They will need to adjust their timing to accommodate this, not to fight it by continuing on with their lines regardless.

Be considerate to others

Don't lurk in the wings and block entrances and exits.

Don't shriek and laugh or chatter or sing anywhere near the stage.

Turn up in good time. Remember that the make-up needs plenty of time and that the stage manager and producer and all the cast will be in a state of panic if you do not drift up until five minutes before your entrance.

Technical rehearsals

The final chapter on practical matters deals in detail with lighting, sound, scenery, make-up and so on and should be referred to for specific information.

The technical rehearsal is very important and ideally there should be more than one, to allow time to experiment and to sort out any hiccups. If the electrics, lighting and other stage technicalities are not given any time or attention before the dress rehearsal, this is likely to turn into highly fraught and exhausting occasion.

There is so much to go wrong and so much that will be all the better for some adjustment and refining. After all, the cast have been rehearsing for weeks to achieve their polish and yet, despite having to hire equipment and inaccessibility of venues, we often expect the technical side simply to slide in smoothly at the last minute.

A first technical rehearsal does not need all the cast, just the guidance of the producer and a few suitable bodies willing to stand in the right positions so that lighting angles, special effects, scene and property changes, sound effects, curtain timing and so on can be tested and adjusted. The aim is to run through the technical aspects of the play in sequence so that they will all be properly coordinated, right from curtain up to finale.

A second dry run may have the luxury of the actual cast but will, once again, be a quick flash-through of positions and cues.

This concentration of time on the technical aspects will pay great dividends later in lessening the frustration and tempers inevitably lost if the dress rehearsal is expected to satisfy the needs of both an over-anxious acting team and a backstage crew that have had no opportunity to use the stage before. Their priorities are of equal weight but different, and it is difficult to keep everyone happy at this time when the tensions and excitement are building up.

The final rehearsal

Keep it happy!

There will be mistakes. There will be some aspects you, as the producer, would like to have improved. There was no time to paint that awning with the proper blue stripes; the hen costume is rather too big; Susan has never really 'milked' that scene properly, no matter how much you discussed it; the green lighting for the cave scene is a bit overdone – perhaps there is still time to adjust. . . The cow is still singing a little too loudly.

You are nit-picking now. The perfectionist wants perfection. As you watch the dress rehearsals, these minor details need to be noted, of course, and corrected if at all possible. But do not overlook the good points too. It is all too easy to rush in to correct the final little errors and forget to tell the cast about the good aspects. So balance out the criticisms and advice with compliments and praise. Make sure when the cast leave that they are optimistic and positive – not complacent or cock-sure, of course, but looking forward to a successful show that will reward all their hard work and effort. Poised to perform!

Stay calm and confident. Encourage and praise, titivate what needs titivating but do not aggravate where there is nothing to be gained. Stay in control and concentrate on what really matters.

Let each act run and then, in between acts, call all the cast and backstage team together to discuss the problems and to listen to your analysis of all the good and bad points. Ensure everyone gathers to listen and that the one person who really needs a rap over the knuckles is not upstairs changing or lurking in the loo having a fag.

Much of this overlaps what will be said about the first night, but then, in a way, the final dress rehearsal should be seen as the first real performance and the standards set for what is to come. It is too late to remind the cast of these things after they have happened. And the first-night audience deserve a polished show. They are not there just to practise on!

Tell the cast that the stage manager is in charge from now on, and is 'the boss', although you will still be around. You are also handing over responsibility directly to the cast and backstage team to make the most of the show, to give the pantomime their very best shot.

Thank everyone for all their efforts and wish them luck.

6

Acting tips and techniques

Communication

It is very easy for actors to become self-centred, to view the pantomime from their angle only – is it a good part? How much do I have to learn? Will there be ample opportunity for me to show off my talents to the full? Am I doing this right? Are we going to finish in time for me to go to the pub? The less selfish actor will sometimes consider the needs and aims of the production as a whole. Does this scene work? How can we improve it? Finally, they may think about the audience, but often only in terms of numbers and whether Fred from work will be suitably impressed with the performance.

Of course, the Freds of this world only arrive at the very end. All the rehearsal time has been carried on in isolation from an audience. Those who happen to be watching out front are likely to be relatives or friends who know a good deal about what is going on because the subject has dominated mealtime conversation for the last six weeks or so. Or they may be committee members who have been in on all the discussions about the choice of script and so on.

Most of the techniques discussed in this section are to help the actor (and to help the producer to help the actor) to communicate to the audience to the best of their combined abilities. Never overlook the needs of the audience, fresh through the door, coming in from the cold and totally unaware of what is going to be thrown at them – sometimes literally! They need to understand what is going on, to know who is who and to follow the story line. Many of them will be children and the pantomime must not ignore their needs. An audience of bored children is lethal.

So remember whom the performance is aimed at: those out front, who have paid to see you. It is not just an exercise to inflate the egos of the cast on stage or a vehicle for a keen lighting person or overenthusiastic choreographer. Ultimately those who are sitting there watching the pantomime need to have a damn good evening out. Help them to do so!

Establishing character

In any production, establishing who you are, what type of person, matters a great deal. The audience need to identify the character quickly and recognise him or her when the actor appears again later. However brief the appearance, the character must be placed firmly in the minds of the audience. In fact, the briefer the appearance, the more vital it is to be a real convincing character from the word 'Go'.

During the performance, there will be costumes and make-up to convey an immediate impression. Some actors never go beyond that; they learn lines and then rely on the trappings to do the rest. But the work should begin at the very first rehearsal. Characters need to be discussed and analysed, experimented with, practised, honed and perfected. Stance, voice, movement, facial expressions and little mannerisms will help to provide an all-round real person rather than just a hollow representation.

Pantomime characters are very vivid, extremes in most cases, and can be an excuse to go over the top. It is up to the director to control the levels and make sure the balance is right.

Having built up a good, strong character during rehearsal, the actor needs to have a few moments before each entrance to think himself back into the part. He or she should assume the role before appearing on stage, and should begin acting in the wings. Pull a few appropriate faces, take up the right stance and think how the character feels at this moment in the play.

Some people are so delighted with their roles, they never switch off at all. Many a dressing room rings to the tones of falsetto voices, booming giants' voices, shrill witches' cackles and rich foreign accents. Great! This is what it is all about.

Moves

Body movement

Anyone who has watched Desmond Morris's television programmes, such as *The Naked Ape*, which examine human society and behaviour, will realise that a good deal of body language is used unconsciously in everyday relationships and human interaction.

Many actors will slip into instinctive body stances and reactions but the fact of standing up on a stage can, for some – especially beginners – freeze these normally automatic responses. Once upon the boards, they become very self-conscious about their bodies, especially hands and feet and unable to control them.

A general rule is always to make any moves as clear, precise and purposeful as possible. Hopping about, hesitating or making short small movements, unless deliberately trying to convey a nervous character, should be avoided.

It is useful to learn to become more aware of body movement and to be able to utilise this understanding once up on the stage rather than being overwhelmed by it.

A useful exercise

A good method of exploring body stance and movement is to let the actors act out a scene while wearing masks to hide their faces and then ask others to analyse what their movements suggest. It is surprising how different these actions will appear when seen in isolation, without the eyes and facial expression conveying additional information. Ask the watching members of the group to tell the masked actor what emotion he or she appears to be indicating; it may not be at all what the actor intended.

Learning to use limbs and gestures more consciously will be a very useful asset and helps to create much more confidence.

Standing still

Standing completely still can add dramatic emphasis to a situation, but it can be one of the most difficult things to do. Even actors not normally subject to foot shuffling or hand wringing can feel awkward if left on the periphery of the action with nothing obvious to do for a long time.

Perhaps because of our inflated egos, we can find it difficult to conceive that the audience might – and indeed should – be concentrating on somebody else: on the actors who are speaking and/or moving at the time. It does take considerable discipline to stand still. Try to reassure those concerned that it does not look unnatural but if they really feel uncomfortable, find them something specific and appropriate to do or they might choose to do something totally out of keeping. The coarse actor can all too easily grab audience attention by picking his nose or yawning or sitting down suddenly at such a time.

Gesticulation

The hands are very important and can express all manner of attitudes and reactions: try hands outspread for pathos and resignation, thumbs up, thumbs down, cocking a snook and so on. Practising in front of a mirror may help. Ask the actors to think about it, and not to make any gestures for gesture's sake; that will be distracting rather than a help.

Facial expressions

Raised eyebrows, frowns, leers, open mouths, pursed lips: these facial expressions are vital and help the actor to feel right but may not always be visible to the back row of the audience. So they must be exaggerated in order to be appreciated. They should complement the more obvious body movement and gesticulation rather than being relied upon as the sole indicators of emotion.

Entrances and exits

In a pantomime it is fun to bring actors through the body of the hall as well having them enter and exit via the conventional means of doorways and wings. This helps the audience feel involved with what is happening and allows for much more variety. Steps at centre front or at the sides of the stage, or both, will allow for more options of access to the stage.

You may or may not wish to maintain the pantomime tradition of 'goodies' entering stage right and 'baddies' stage left. For purely practical reasons, such as lighting in special colours, this can be useful, and the audience quite enjoy the anticipation of action in these areas once they have accepted the convention.

Entering through trap doors or suspending actors on wires will not generally be options on the small amateur stage, but there are other ways to make dramatic entrances. For instance, if there is sufficient wing space, a genie can be catapulted into action off a small trampoline or leap in from a raised block. Combined with a jet of smoke and a coloured flash, this can be quite exciting.

In general, it is important that entrances and exits are exploited so that they can be as much fun and as lively as possible, helping to establish character and adding to the overall drama of the story when appropriate. Use your imagination, think laterally, ask others for their ideas and it is surprising what can be achieved. If all else fails, send up the desired action. I once 'flew' Tinkerbell by having actors run behind her carrying moving clouds, their legs hidden by a solid low wall of cloud. Wearing a flying helmet and goggles and elegantly flapping her wings to the music of *The Dam Busters*, she made a superb entrance. So far as the actor is concerned, the main aim is to make a strong, confident entrance, to be in character even before setting foot on stage and not to bump into anyone else.

Voice

As already discussed in the audition section, the voice is a very important element of stage performance and helps enormously to establish character.

Ask a man to be a dame or a giant or a dandy and he will instantly assume an appropriate voice. In a similar way, players who are enacting animals will generally miaow or bark or grunt or moo and think about how to reflect the particular creature in the way they enunciate words. Some people are much better than others at changing their voices but often it is simply a factor that is overlooked. It should be just as important for those who are playing straight roles to consider how a change or inflection of voice might render their characterisation more distinct. The hero and heroine, the bystander and the fairy need to try out different deliveries too – just like the dame.

Accent and intonation

Consider using regional accents – country yokel, Scottish, Welsh, Irish, Brummy, Lancashire, Yorkshire, Cockney, Liverpudlian and so on. Or foreign accents from anywhere around the globe, from America to Australia, Sweden to India – but only, of course, as appropriate to the part concerned. And not too many different accents in one pantomime or the audience will be understandably baffled by an overcooked international approach.

A silly comic voice (usually sustainable only for brief appearances) can change the interpretation of a character completely. You can also try:

change of pitch (falsetto, soprano, high and squeaky, deep bass)
sweet coarse and rasping, harsh or shrill
lisp
stutter
upper-crust
staccato
strangled
fruity
breathy
gutteral
droning
bellowing
shrieking
sing song

The point is that there is an enormous variety of sound to play with, often largely ignored. And it really can make an enormous difference.

Don't force the issue if an actor cannot cope and loses confidence when he or she feels that an accent or change of voice is forced. But do experiment. Often a new voice can help a character to take shape in the same way that costumes make a person feel completely different.

And it isn't always the obvious voice to go for. A macho supergenie in one production of Aladdin made a stunning appearance. He arrived in a puff of smoke and stood grandly poised on the stage with his arms folded in true genie fashion. He looked very powerful, from his Oriental pigtail to his Superman boots. So when he suddenly broke the spell by speaking with a *Goon Show* Neddy voice, the audience convulsed into giggles. It was a wonderful unexpected twist – a joke that depended entirely on the choice of voice and did not exist in the original script.

Diction and audibility

Whatever else the audience deserve, having paid their entrance fees, one of the essentials is that they should be able to understand what is happening. To do this, apart from when they are watching slapstick or visual scenes, they need to be able to hear what the actors are saying to them and to each other.

Some actors simply will not speak up, no matter what you say or how much you encourage them. Learning to throw the voice is not easy, especially for the beginner or someone with a very quiet voice. It needs a lot of practice and it is no good deciding there is a problem at the last dress rehearsal. Use all the rehearsal time available to develop the skills. Don't ignore the problem and hope the actor will rise to the occasion once there is an audience. Not only is this policy unlikely to work, but the actors who make a sudden last-ditch effort are likely to strain their voices and end up losing them by the end of the run. The Saturday night audience will not appreciate the entire performance being rendered in strangled whispers.

Speaking too fast is a common problem and it can take considerable discipline to slow down if you are naturally a fast speaker. The problem is often exacerbated when an actor is nervous or puts down the script for the first time. There is a subconscious desire to hurtle through all the words at top speed in the hope that the end might just be reached before the lines are quite forgotten again.

Most rehearsal schedules do not allow for much time to be spent on relaxation and workshop exercises to combat such problems, unless the actors want to try them in between their bouts on stage. So the producer should make sure everyone learns the lines in good time, and then constant nagging of the gabblers and plenty of practice are really the best policy.

Remember that it is important to keep the volume up when actors turn their backs on the audience, exit into the wings while still speaking or when moving down into the audience. Actors need to compensate more than they might imagine. Make sure everyone is aware of this.

Sometimes volume drops for no good reason. Perhaps the actor is simply tired or not concentrating or thinks it is not worth bothering during the rehearsal. Perhaps he or she has a cold. Whatever, do find out why it is happening. Talk about it.

Timing and pace

This is a vital part of the production process. Speed, without loss of audibility or integrity, is a skill that can be practised. For some, a good sense of timing seems to be a natural gift; others need to be helped. Largely, it is a case of thoroughly understanding the script and its intended effect on the audience at any moment. If actors are too fast or too slow, killing punch lines, pausing too long or not pausing at all when they should, do not just tell them to do it differently – tell them why they should do it differently. And, if time allows, experiment a little with delivery and moves to see what a huge difference they make.

Improvisation

Improvisation too comes more easily to some actors than to others. Bear this in mind when you cast: certain roles, especially humorous parts or 'link men', require more improvisation than others.

It is largely a matter of confidence and there are many techniques which will help to improve this, from relaxation exercises to morale-boosting chats, but the biggest help of all is really thorough rehearsal.

A certain amount of improvisation can be anticipated. The good actor or director will know which pieces of action or dialogue are likely to provoke the audience to interact with the play and some 'improvised' lines can be prepared, just in case. For example, if the starting pistol proves unreliable in rehearsal, have an amusing line ready about the gun's silencer. The joy of pantomime is that such mishaps – which in a conventional play might ruin the climax – can instead be turned to your advantage.

But there are always moments for which no one can be ready, such as one occasion when a stray ginger cat decided to wander through the audience and up the steps to the stage. There was a camel acting up there at the time and Humpthree promptly welcomed his new ginger friend with much warmth and affection, remarking upon the sad loss of his new colleague's humps and telling him that we were doing *Puss in Boots* next year.

It is important to ad lib in character, of course. On another occasion two actors in a clinging embrace became trapped together when the gentleman's buttons caught in the lady's lace blouse. After struggling to separate and soon realising the impossibility of this, Bob remarked, in suitable Restoration manner:

> 'Madam, how is't we are thus entangled? Forsooth, 'tis plain thou canst not bear to be set asunder from neither my personage nor my apparel. Gadzooks! We must go hither, ever tied in love's sweet knot.'

The pair then lurched sideways through the wings, rather like a three-legged crab race.

Slapstick

Some people are natural buffoons. The techniques of visual comedy can be learned, acquired, imparted – but it helps if there is natural clown in your midst. Add a 'straight man' and you will have the basic raw ingredients for knockabout humour.

The word 'slapstick' itself implies a degree of violence and it is this close proximity to discomfiture – whether pain, abuse, injury or loss of dignity – that is the strange root of humour. Slapstick is all about uncomfortable and painful experiences – which we all fear – being ridiculed and, above all, happening to somebody else.

However, because of the underlying threat of violence, it is vital to get the mix right or the audience will shrink from the unpleasant aspects and will not enjoy the show at all. Introduce too realistic blood or heart-rending screams and the humour will die instantly. It is necessary to strike a careful balance between the two faces of humour: the cruel and the comic.

Slapstick has been described as 'the comedy of action' and its protagonists as comedians who 'make their living by falling down, not as *stand-up* comics'. Natural clowns are pretty athletic performers but learning to fall properly and without injury is quite a specialised skill and many pantomime amateurs can be quite badly bruised if the antics are too demanding. It helps to use a mattress or some soft landing place if possible. Since slapstick is such visual humour, minimal dialogue is required, although of course an apt comment will serve to underline the humour – as did the explanatory sentences in the old silent-movie routines.

If the pantomime follows an existing script, then a slapstick scene may well be described in detail, but if you are writing your own script or introducing your own knockabout comedy scene into an existing script, it will help to observe good comic scenes in other productions, in the theatre or on film or television, and to analyse their humour. Live theatre, especially pantomime, has the great advantage over film or television of audience feedback, which can help the humour enormously.

Do not make it too long

Slapstick scenes, like stage fights, require a good deal of rehearsal to run smoothly and it is better to do a very short scene really well than to overextend one. Good timing is absolutely crucial and will require close coordination between the actors. A five-minute sketch may take several hours of rehearsal to be truly effective. A rushed job will be weak. Allow time to experiment and consolidate. A superb comedian may well be able to ad lib and introduce extra humour spontaneously, but the backbone of the scene must be rock solid.

Involve the backstage team right from the start

Slapstick scenes often require the backup of trick scenery and props. Involve the whole team, not just the actors, and draw on their know-how and suggestions. The humour will rely in part on suitable equipment and tricks, even if only custard pies. Ample preparation time and trial and error will help to iron out any deficiencies and maximise the effectiveness of the props.

Use the natural comics

I have known many a fairly tedious scene, not actually intended to be comic, to become hilarious, the highlight of the show, by the introduction of a natural comedian, perhaps initially on the fringes of the real action.

In one melodramatic scene where a rendering of a long-winded Victorian poem was quite obviously going to stretch the tolerance of the audience, I introduced a 'natural' to help the scene along with some 'special effects'. He was to follow the orator with a stepladder and a bucket filled with 'rain', 'snow' or whatever else might be tipped on to the orator and be appropriate to the content of the poem. Complete with a handkerchief into which to sob when the most poignant moments were reached, this particular comedian completely stole the scene, to the delight of all concerned. He managed to make the stepladder fairly dance across the stage in pursuit of the poor actor trying to give a serious, straight-faced rendition and it was howlingly funny.

Involve the audience

Many a slapstick scene is made even more amusing by luring up on the stage one or two members of the audience. This helps the audience to feel that they are part of the game. Moreover, the remaining members of the audience are so relieved not to be the victims up on stage that it makes them laugh all the more at what is going on up there. The victims can help bake a cake, be sung to, play party games, try on Cinderella's slipper, dance the can-can or whatever is appropriate. If the slapstick scene is messy it would be unkind to make them victims of the custard-pie element, but a few near-misses will add to the humour considerably.

Similarly, throwing things into the audience, whether for real or as a false alarm, can generate gales of laughter.

Do not forget to allow ample opportunity for the basic pantomime-audience responses: 'Look out behind you' and 'Oh no, I didn't' – 'Oh yes, you did'. Children soon catch on to what is expected of them and when they are joining in they will laugh all the more at funny situations – for example, when someone is creeping up behind another actor and then constantly turning in unison with the person in front so as not to be seen.

General comedy and humour

Slapstick is only one element of pantomime humour. Most of the techniques of conveying humour and making an audience laugh will apply to all comedy scenes, slapstick or otherwise.

Relaxing the audience

Get the audience involved from the moment they walk in. Make the hall festive, if possible with some of the set encroaching beyond the confines of the proscenium arch. In one revue with a seaside theme we had a photographer there to take photographs of people putting their heads through full-size seaside postcard scenes while they waited for the play to start, so there was lots of laughter before the play even began. Seaside music, along with the sound of waves and seagulls, helped to provide a relaxing holiday atmosphere.

People will laugh most readily when they are relaxed and happy or, contrarily, when they are nervous. It is the happy laughter you are seeking generally, although the nervous reaction can be capitalised on as well on occasions. To relax the audience, they need to be warmed up first, and this can be achieved in various ways.

Once the audience is laughing, this will catch and spread. It is always wonderful when one member of the audience with an especially infectious laugh sets off the rest of them. If one of the cast who laughs naturally and easily can do so up on stage as part of the action, these bouts of mirth will help the audience along – like the canned laughter in television programmes.

Partners and duos

Often in pantomime, it is the dame or dames (like the Ugly Sisters in *Cinderella*) who will dominate the humorous scenes. Still, whichever characters are involved, try to find teams that get on well together and will manage to extract the maximum humour out of the scenes because of their teamwork.

The classic comedy team is the clown and the straight man. Think of Laurel and Hardy, Morecambe and Wise, the two Ronnies, Cannon and Ball. It is not necessarily the scenes they are enacting that are so amusing, but rather the interaction between them, the contrasting attitudes and expressions that can render even fairly pedestrian situations hysterically funny.

It may not be easy to discover such ideal partners. Perfect comedy duos are probably made in heaven and possibly more difficult to find than perfect marriage partners. But it is fairly straightforward to highlight contrasting physical characteristics – tall and short; fat and thin – or to exaggerate opposing attitudes; pessimistic and optimistic; happy and sad; efficient and clumsy; serious and funny; clever and stupid; refined and coarse. Such foils will add to the humour enormously.

Strengthen the visual element

Add to the buffoonery by exaggerating the body movements: waving arms, silly walks, running in circles, shrugging shoulders and so on. Children love the ridiculous and pantomime allows actors to indulge in exaggerated action such as the high-stepping tiptoe used by villains up to no good. Creeping secretly, sssshhhing and looking back over the shoulder, especially if well-rehearsed and done in perfect unison by a few players, is always amusing.

Emphasis to a situation can also be greatly increased by gesticulation. In fact, everything that was discussed generally at the beginning of this chapter with regard to general movement on the stage is especially important in comedy and in the 'silent movie' of visual humour.

This has just scratched the surface of acting techniques. For those who want to know more, there are many specialist books on the subject and courses to take. Every little bit of knowledge helps and improves the general pool of know-how within the group.

7

Music, dance and crowd scenes

However limited the musical talents of the producer and society members seem, it is important to include music in a pantomime. Some song and dance will add colour and variety to the show and help to underline dramatic situations. Provided the actors can sing reasonably well and keep in tune, confidence rather than expertise is the main ingredient, and, anyway, everyone improves with encouragement and practice.

The society may be blessed with evident musical talent, members who have announced that they are willing to sing or play the trumpet or guitar. Once a group has a reputation for doing musical shows, it will attract these keen performers. However, if the musical element is a new one, there may not yet be an established pool of talent.

Even if there are established singers within the group, never overlook the potential abilities of the other members. And if no one wants to sing at all, then you will have to search out the talent. People can be very shy about their vocal attributes and may need coaxing to admit that they are willing to have a go, and quite a lot of further confidence boosting before they will actually perform solo songs.

Stick to chorus work if that is all you feel the group can manage first time around, but listen in to the chorus singing around the piano to try and discover good voices. Let people sing in small groups or pairs if they really dare not go it alone. And, if possible, let newly fledged solo artists have some relatively private practice with the pianist until they have learned the basic tune or tunes reasonably well. This makes sense anyway because you do not want to waste the general time on a single person's learning process.

Lots and lots of practice will overcome initial nervousness. This really is vital for nerves will make the voice shake and squeak, cause breathlessness, inability to hit the right notes and possible loss of lines – an unnerving experience in performance because it is well-nigh impossible to prompt a song.

Good breathing, learning to use the diaphragm properly and relaxation exercises will help. However, often the performers will tell you later that singing to the rest of the team for the first time was far more nerve-racking than performing to the audience. Reassure them on this score when they first stand up and sing in front of the others: 'Well done, Helen! That sounded lovely. And I promise you it will never be so difficult again. Now you've faced this mob, the audience will be a doddle!' Wean beginners off the private lessons and get them singing in normal rehearsals as soon as possible so that it becomes second nature, not some big deal.

During the show, especially if under a spotlight, one can feel almost as alone as when singing in the bath – but the applause is better!

At the other end of the scale from the nervous good singers are the dreadful singers who *think* they are good and belt out an off-key rendering with great gusto. Those who know that they are tone deaf and opt out voluntarily are no problem, but if the singer is oblivious to his or her ineptitude it is more difficult. Wrong notes undermine the whole chorus and can make it difficult for the in-key singers to hold their own, especially if they are not certain of the tune yet. Anyway, it sounds dreadful. First detect the culprit or culprits. Then they need to be taken aside and tactfully asked to refrain – or given some other task to perform that will preclude their singing.

Copyright

In an ideal world, you will discover in your midst a budding composer and a lyricist who can put Andrew Lloyd Webber and Tim Rice in the shade. This does not happen very often, but do ask around and see just who can do what. If there is someone who likes composing music and the standard really is good enough, then grab this person, who will probably be flattered and delighted to be given an opportunity for his or her compositions to have a public airing.

It is more likely, however, that you will want to perform music that already exists. It may have been composed as an integral part of the pantomime you have purchased, or you may bring in existing music that suits your needs. In fact, familiar music is good because the audience enjoy tunes that they recognise. It is also easier for the cast to learn.

Even if the music is affiliated to the pantomime, it may be subject to separate licence, royalties and copyright. Double-check the paperwork from whoever supplied the script and the small print in the play copies.

If you are introducing musical numbers from other sources, even if you are altering the tune and changing the words, you will certainly need to clear copyright and obtain permission for performance. The best people to help are the Performing Rights Society, who can advise on who owns the copyright and needs to be contacted. Their address and telephone number are on page 24.

Musical director and orchestra

A full-bloodied musical director who takes over directing the musical numbers will help enormously, particularly if the producer is no musician. If the producer is totally without musical know-how, then delegation is the only way.

A good pianist and accompanist will be able to teach the cast the songs, guide the singers through rehearsals, point out when the notes or rhythm are wrong and generally support the producer throughout the musical rehearsals.

It helps if the pianist can play new music on sight and pull tunes out of the air on request. But if your accompanist is not thus gifted, it is up to you to give him or her plenty of time to practise first. Familiarity with the music will, in any case, help even the most talented pianist to interpret the songs more appropriately and give singers the most effective support.

Music is a vital element of pantomime, however small the 'orchestra'.

If the pianist has not accompanied singers before but only performed solo, he or she will need to get used to being constantly interrupted, to following the voices and being sensitive to the needs of the cast, playing more quietly for weaker voices, and pitching the music correctly. At the first music rehearsal, the cast always argue that the key needs to be changed – the songs are far too high, they complain – but by the end of the rehearsal period, with all the extra practice, most of the cast can reach the notes quite happily. Often they believe the key has been pitched lower when it has, in fact, remained at its original level.

Extra instruments can help to make a good all-round musical sound, but unless microphones and speakers are used – which can be a mixed blessing and singularly inappropriate in, for example, medieval England – make sure the voices are not drowned. Drummers, in particular, can be carried away, playing far too loudly for a small hall, and may need to be restricted to brushes. Drums will help enormously, though, to give a professional sound and to keep the rhythm flowing. They are useful for percussion sound effects too – rolling of drums and cymbal clashes when the dame falls over, and so on.

Gather in what you can – violins, guitars, double bass, trumpet, trombones or whatever – but bear in mind that the orchestra has to work as a whole and that, like the chorus, the more there are of them, the greater the rehearsal and coordination problems may be. So make sure they can all work together happily and constructively and that there are no prima donnas trying to take over. If the venue is small and seating restricted, do check that there is sufficient room to accommodate the potential orchestra without losing too many precious audience seats.

Dance sequences

As with the singing, when it comes to dance and choreography it is always helpful if you can draw on available local expertise. Most towns, however small, have their own ballet or dance school. Teachers are generally delighted to give their youngsters a chance to perform, provided the dates do not clash with examinations or a show of their own. Make sure everyone has lots of notice and agrees to the commitment officially in good time so there are no last-minute panics. Discuss your needs clearly, the type of dance, the dates involved, costumes and so on, so that the lines of responsibility are clearly stated and understood. There are many reasons why this may not be practical, however. A clash of dates, geography (if the local dance class is miles away) and the casting of the pantomime which may mean that the dancers definitely have to come from within the ranks. In this case, it may be preferable to bring the expertise into your own rehearsals and keep everything under your control. If there is a local teacher who is willing to take on rank beginners from your society, then let her or him loose on the rabble – with your sympathy and blessing!

This may not work, either. Perhaps the dance instructor is too busy or simply uncooperative. It happens. So you are on your own. Should you abandon the notion of dance? That would be a pity, since it does introduce another magic ingredient into the show. But then again, bad dancing is worse, if anything, than bad singing, so you may decide simply to abandon the idea.

Before taking this step, consider putting out an SOS. First ask the assembled cast. It is almost certain that one or two of them have some kind of dancing skills and can put a few dance steps together quite satisfactorily. If there is just one 'expert' in your midst, this may be all you need.

Alternatively, somebody in the society may know someone else who can help. Or an advertisement can be placed in the local press. The only problem with a cooperative venture from within the cast is that if there are too many ideas and too many bosses, it can lead to arguments. It is essential to establish who is in charge so that there are no disputes. This is especially important if the person who knows most is very young and can therefore feel a little intimidated at the thought of supervising older members. In any case the producer should get together with the choreographer first and establish precisely what is required.

However expert the choreographer, the producer will need to approve the routines at some stage and bring to bear his or her knowledge of moves and chorus work – which are not so very different from looking at a dance sequence. The intricacy of steps, the need to tie in closely with the music and the range of terminology will be greater but the overall aim is much the same as that of conventional moves – to create the right atmosphere, to move well, to move together, and not to knock each other or the scenery over.

Always make sure that the dance routines suit the abilities of the dancers; do not push your luck with complete beginners. Keep it as simple as possible unless there are experienced dancers who justify more ambitious ideas.

Crowd and choral scenes

Crowd scenes have been included in this chapter because in pantomime they are generally the chorus and therefore going to be making a very important contribution to the music. It can work well to bring in a choreographer to oversee difficult crowd or chorus sections, even if no dancing is involved at all. Moving a crowd scene is a choreographic exercise, whether during a song or a dialogue. It is one of the most difficult things to do effectively, especially if the number of people is large and the stage is small.

In addition to this, it needs only flu to strike, or other unforseen circumstances – and suddenly you discover that there will never be a rehearsal with the full chorus altogether until the final dress rehearsal. The greater the number involved, the greater the risk of this occurring.

This seems like an impossible situation to manage but if the producer is well organised and the scenes are carefully planned and structured, it is not as bad as it sounds. The jigsaw pieces can be made to fit together once the full team is finally gathered.

Moving the masses

The chapter on planning ahead discusses how to plan moves, using miniature charts of the stage and drawing in lines and circles to represent each character (see pages 30-1). This can become very complicated when there are perhaps twenty or thirty people milling about, so give yourself plenty of time to work it all outbeforehand. It will be chaotic if you arrive at a crowd scene rehearsal totally unprepared. For now you are like a general with an impending battle ahead and you need to have some idea how to draw up the battle lines, how to use the cavalry and how to place your strongest forces in order to use them to best advantage.

With these numbers of people to control, you will not really be able to draw lines to represent all the details of routes that individuals take without creating a tangled, incomprehensible cobweb. However, in some instances you will be moving them as groups, and you can then treat the group rather as you would a single actor.

When there is a very complicated criss-crossing of individual actors, the only way to cope is to have many copies of the stage plan and then just mark their various positions, rather than their routes, as related to dialogue or lyrics. Draw separately or write in words a note about any particularly difficult or 'woven' routes. Impress on the actors concerned that you expect them to have sufficient intelligence and memory to keep track of their own movements and route. It is easier for them to remember one set of moves than for you to carry thirty sets in your head. However, because of the inevitable missing bodies and the fact that some of those standing up there will still forget where to go, you do need your notes.

Then, of course, when they are all actually moving up there and the music is flowing, you discover that since you mapped it all out, Selina and Brian have dropped out of this scene, there are too many people to get up the steps in the time you envisaged, the giant's castle has had to move from its original position and anyway, that inept circling round the beanstalk looks *awful*!

So you will change your mind. Probably there will be a good number of revisions before the moves all interlock neatly, look good, fit the music and flow smoothly. Do keep note of the changes. This is where an assistant is of particular use, because otherwise you will find that you are scribbling away like mad instead of watching the stage.

It can help to give the actors numbers. Figures take up less space on your notes and if there is a vital order in which the actors appear, it helps to be able to call out and orchestrate the entrances. Once people are up there you will probably revert to names instinctively, however: '1 and 2 , 3 and 4 – from the upstage wings, please – 5 and 6, 7 and 8 – in from the downstage wings now. 9 and 10 – where are you, 9 and 10? You should be coming up the steps now! 11, 12 and 13 – enter through the hall and down the centre aisle. 7 and 8 – Peter and Jane – you should have reached the beanstalk by now! 14 and 15, in through the castle doors at the back. Harry and Sue, you were meant to have moved across to talk to Angela long before this! 16, 17, 18 and 19, in through the upstage wings. no, no, no – not all from the same side! 16 and 17 stage left; 18 and 19 stage right. Sally, you, are blocking the dame's entrance – move further left. 20 and 21, through the hall and stand on top of the side steps. 22 – through the castle gate. Right, everyone mingle and chat and then take up your positions for the first line of the song. Right, let's try that again – with the intro music this time.'

Absenteeism and stand-ins

Absenteeism can cause chaos in crowd scenes like this. It is essential to have stand-ins so that you can check that it really does all work, and for this you can drum up any actors not involved in the scene – or the prompt, or Sally's mother who's just arrived to watch, or the caretaker!

Other actors will undoubtedly move better than an unsuspecting novice press-ganged into action – but there are disadvantages. The main danger of using other actors as stand-ins, whether in crowd scenes or not, is that it seems to be an unwritten law of amateur dramatics that whoever you ask to stand in always has an entrance of their own in two minutes and ends up disappearing into their proper role or diving from one side of the stage to the other, being two people at once. Besides, you frequently find yourself rebuking these poor willing souls for standing in the wrong place when they know no better because it is not actually their part at all – but you have forgotten that in the mayhem. And then the following week you tell the 'real' actors off for getting it wrong and they quite rightly protest, 'But I wasn't here last week and you had me standing stage left last time. I've got it written down here quite clearly.'

Stay calm, keep notes, ensure the cast write everything down as well and somehow, if everyone works hard to help you along, it does all come together in time and the eventual result looks good. The worst thing is the waste of time for everybody if the move-learning has to be repeated too often, so if actors do turn out to be thoroughly unreliable, read the riot act, do not use them again if things do not improve, and drop them from the show entirely if there is no other way to make it work.

Never underestimate the importance of the crowd scene roles

Impress on the whole team that crowd scenes and chorus are *very, very* important parts. They are not just given out as compensation for not landing a major role. If anything, the complications of having to coordinate with large numbers of other people requires enormous self-discipline and is more demanding than many solo roles. Getting it right means *everyone* getting it right, not just one person, so it can take a lot of rehearsal and control and repetition.

Never let anyone think that an inept or unreliable soul can be 'lost' in the chorus. One person doing something badly, in a group that is otherwise professional and disciplined, stands out only too clearly and undermines the whole effect.

Actors often labour under the illusion that if they miss chorus or music rehearsals, this is not such a heinous crime as missing their speaking bits. Part of the pep talk in Rehearsal One should emphasise that this is not the case and is a very selfish and foolish attitude. They will certainly be missed, their absence will infuriate their fellow actors and anyway, they need all the time allocated in order to learn what is required.

In the same way, learning the words of songs is as important as learning spoken lines. Lurking at the back, opening and closing mouths like goldfish, pretending to sing; coming in a fraction later than everybody else in order to crib the words; hiding scripts in the back row; or singing the wrong words entirely against the flow – this kind of thing needs to be stamped out immediately. If everyone thinks that someone else can learn the words first to make it easier to follow, nobody in fact, learns them at all.

Throughout all this, as you watch the stage, analyse exactly what the crowd are meant to be feeling and what they are adding to the dramatic element. Make sure the moves, the shape and patterns of the bodies on the stage, the individual expressions on faces, the voices and the overall mood all convey this accurately, and that the atmosphere is given stronger emphasis by what the crowd are doing. For example, it might be:

a welcoming opening – make sure they smile
bustling and busy – lots of movement needed
a joyous celebration – cheers and smiles
frightened – exchanged whispers, looking over shoulders
confused – shrugging shoulders, exchanging blank looks
angry and threatening – waving arms, shaking fists, shouts
ominous – sullen silences, knowing looks

If it is a happy scene, they need to smile, even when singing, as much as possible – although one producer I worked with was told in no uncertain terms where she could jump when she asked one section of the chorus to 'Smile, for goodness sake!' when they were in the middle of whistling the tune.

Good acting is just as important for those in the crowds as for solo parts and, if done well, creates a rich and effective tapestry on the stage.

8

Audience participation

First impressions: a warm welcome

The atmosphere in the hall matters from the moment the audience arrive at the door. Make it as welcoming as possible. One of the thrills of going to a theatre is that excited buzz in the foyer, everybody dressed up, programmes for sale and the hum of anticipation as you enter the auditorium. Every time I hear an orchestra tuning up in readiness for a show and then see the curtain rise, I still feel the same thrill of excitement, no matter how often I go.

It can be hard to create the same feeling in a draughty hall with hard seats and curtains that look tired and tatty. If this is the kind of venue in which the drama society has to perform, the members need to think carefully about how to improve matters. They may not have any say in the matter of the hall's decoration or seating but gentle pools of light, a welcoming warmth, music playing and cheerful, smiling faces can help greatly to improve matters.

Put up some photographs of past productions, of this pantomime in rehearsal and close-ups of the cast. Posters and programmes from previous shows and press cuttings will all help to whet the appetite and demonstrate a professional approach. Make the hall look as interesting and lively as possible.

A bevy of helpers to sell programmes, show the audience to their seats, sell raffle tickets and generally be helpful and courteous will set the right tone.

Every pantomime has a particular flavour, whether a historical period or an exciting setting, and the helpers can be dressed appropriately – medieval for *Dick Whittington* or *Babes in the Wood*, wigs and flounces for *Cinderella*, nursery rhyme characters for *Humpty Dumpty*, pirates and grass skirts for *Robinson Crusoe* and *Peter Pan*, Arabian style for *Ali Baba* or Chinese for *Aladdin*.

Ideally these themes should extend beyond the proscenium arch so that the audience are part of the atmosphere right from the moment when they walk in. Audiences who go to see Andrew Lloyd Webber's *Cats* step into the auditorium and find themselves in the middle of a huge rubbish tip, with everything giant-sized so as to be in proportion to the cats. This is great fun and there is plenty to see and talk about before the play begins. Related activities can be purely for fun or a fee can be charged which helps to swell the coffers. Try to find appropriate ideas for the particular pantomime, such as:

Dick Whittington street sellers from medieval London
Babes in the Wood Robin Hood's merry men selling raffle tickets and claiming that they
   are robbing the rich
Hansel and Gretel witches selling licorice allsorts and barley sugar
Snow White children dressed as dwarfs, a magic mirror, witches selling combs and apples

Pinocchio jugglers, stilt walkers, people dressed as animals for a circus theme might suit
this story but could be suitable for several play openings

Jack and the Beanstalk giant-sized objects around the hall, or a country market atmosphere;
with food and produce for sale – perhaps the odd scrawny cow and magic beans, as well

Robinson Crusoe girls dressed in hula skirts bedecking the audience with garlands of flowers

Such activities can take place in the intervals too, of course.

If parts of the scenery can be extended at the sides so it remains visible when the
curtains are drawn, this will help the atmosphere at the beginning and maintain the
magic and audience interest when scenes are performed in front of the curtain line.
We once took fairground scenery right around the hall sides with life-size stalls and
carousel horses. Had there been space, we could have incorporated a real coconut
shy and candy-floss stall. We did sell toffee apples in the interval!

However you go about it, make the audience feel part of the show from the
moment they step in off the pavement.

Food and wine

A cabaret atmosphere can work very well. This can be helped by to seating the
audience around tables rather than in straight rows of chairs. Our society's latest
ploy is to ply the audience with alcohol (one free glass for starters and more
available to buy). Waiters and waitresses refill the glasses or sell whole bottles.
Supper is served and more bottles of wine are sold at a fairly early interval. There
is free orange squash for the children. The audience are always much more relaxed
after conversation, food and drink.

If possible, the food served is appropriate to the theme of the show, with extras
available, labelled according to the characters: Baron Hard-up's Mean Chocolate
Cake, Tinkerbell's Fairy Cakes, Cheese by courtesy of Buttercup the Cow, Dame
Twankey's Tarts, Hansel and Gretel's Gingerbread, Friar Tuck's Sausages and
so on.

The programme

This is one of the means by which you involve the audience before curtain up.
Make sure it is lively and reasonably well produced. It gives a professional edge to
the evening if the programme is on decent paper, is well laid out and includes a
lively introduction to the entertainment that is to come. If it also contains some
games or a lucky number, this may encourage more people to buy one.

Start with a bang

The importance of a good beginning cannot be stressed too often. Capture the
audience straight away. Those first few moments can make them feel, 'Wow! This
is going to be good!' or 'Oh, God! I knew I should have stayed at home and watched
the telly.' Make sure you get the first reaction!

Help them to join in quickly by active involvement, whether joining in a song,
standing up and sitting down again several times, cheering, clapping, playing some
kind of game, booing the villain or doing something silly. For example, suggest that
the audience stand up, turn round and shake hands with the person behind them.

Since everyone is then facing someone's back, this proves an impossible request to fulfil and the ensuing laughter helps to break down the remnants of their reserve.

Inviting the audience to join in a familiar song is a good way to warm them up. The classic community sing-along procedure is as follows:

1. Go through the number reasonably slowly.
2. Tell the audience they are pathetic and need to sing louder.
3. Divide up the two halves of the audience and set them in competition against each other.
4. Divide them up in other ways – male and female, adult and child, those who have bought a raffle ticket and the rotten ones who haven't.
5. Ask them to join in with a rendering of 'My Bonnie Lies Over the Ocean'. The joy of this particular song is that at the end, you ask them all to stand up and then sit down again every time they sing a word beginning with the letter B. By the time they have finished all the 'Bring back's in the chorus, you can guarantee they will be in hysterics.
6. Suggest they give themselves a well-earned round of applause.

Natural comperes and comedians

Whether it is sing-along, a party game or just a short filler while scenery is changed, much depends on the repartee of those on stage. Direct audience participation is most successful when the performers who spearhead the fun are relaxed and confident. Some people are much better than others at improvisation and patter. Put your strongest team forward for these roles – just one person or several together, or a whole range of different people throughout the evening. Of course, the choice will depend on who is available and not halfway inside a change of costume at the time, so do consider this factor when casting.

Between the scenes and emergencies

Quite often, there will be a panic during the dress rehearsal when someone discovers that changing in time is likely to give them a coronary – or that a scene change is much more complicated than anticipated and requires a few extra minutes. It is useful to have a few 'fillers' up your sleeve for these occasions. A stage extension will allow this entertainment to occupy the area in front of the curtains while scenery is changed behind.

If the story has a medieval setting, as many pantomimes do, hand out newspapers to the audience and award a prize for the best medieval hat. Or, as suits the play and development of the story, Oriental, cowboy, Robin Hood, pirate or wedding hats can be created.

Still using newspapers, another very amusing game is to invite eight members of the audience up on the stage or extension and tell them they are travelling in a packed tube train – or farm cart, stage coach, Batmobile, whatever is appropriate. Place them in a confined, squashed, knees-together, arm-jostling formation as shown on page 89. Then provide each contestant with a broadsheet newspaper. (These papers need not be identical but each one should have the same number of pages.) These newspapers will have been previously prepared: the pages jumbled up, upside down, back to front and in total confusion. The winner is the first person to rearrange his or her newspaper into the correct order. It is funny enough to inflict on the rest of the audience because the contestants will soon be crashing

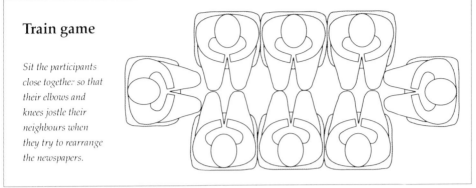

Train game

Sit the participants close together so that their elbows and knees jostle their neighbours when they try to rearrange the newspapers.

Train game: these kind of party games make useful fillers between difficult scene changes.

elbows into a mass of waving arms and papers, and then inevitably start cheating and snatching each other's pages until newsprint and insults are flying in all directions.

It is worth investing in a book of party games so that the society always has one to hand and can figure out which other games are transferable on to the stage. An extra game up your sleeve for emergencies on the night is always a good idea. I hope your production is so well organised and smooth, that emergency cover will never be required, but should one of the cast break an ankle rushing down the stairs from the dressing room, or the curtains jam and refuse to open, or Cinderella's coach come off its wheels immediately before it is needed – then keeping the audience happy and busy will buy a few extra minutes. In the event of a minor catastrophe, there will be less panic and pressure; everyone will remain relatively calm and solve the problems far more quickly because of this.

The audience love to be involved and their participation in a game can be a useful filler between scene changes.

Classic pantomime exchanges

If these are not already included in the scripts, find a suitable spot to insert them. For if *you* do not, your audience doubtless will – and it is always best to be prepared and in control so that the timing is right and the situations are enjoyably milked. Otherwise, the lines may be simply thrown away and the action awkward through lack of rehearsal. The most familiar exchanges include the following:

Booing, hissing, aahs and cheers

A well played villain should always provoke a good audience reaction. A slow audience can be encouraged at the beginning by suitable notices to spur them on and then the villain can sneer, scowl, shake his fist, swirl his cloak if he has one and generally provoke yet more booing and cries of 'Shame!', 'Scoundrel' and so on – in true Victorian melodramatic fashion.

Aah's of sympathy for the heroine can also be prompted by boards – as can clapping, yeses and noes, laughter, cheers, sobs and other outward displays of emotion.

'Look out behind you!' 'Oh no, he isn't!' 'Oh yes, he is!'

These shouts to and fro between audience and cast are an essential ingredient of pantomime, passed down from generation to generation, with the grown-ups first leading the chants and then the children taking them up with increasing gusto. Children really enjoy being invited to help friendly or comic characters with whom they can sympathise – such as Buttons, the dame or the village idiot – by letting them know if someone or something that frightens them is in the vicinity. The scary person or creature needs to be amusing and grinning about the game being played, rather than overpoweringly threatening, or the joke will be spoiled by terrifying the smallest members of the audience.

Prompted by such lines as 'If that big spider (or the gorilla or the ghost) arrives, you will tell me, won't you?' the children will shout out as the spider arrives, unseen by the protagonist in this scene. The spider can hide in various places, changing swiftly from one place to another as the hero desperately enquires: 'Where? Over here? No, he's not. . . Where is he, you say? Over here? No, he's not. . . You're kidding me, aren't you? He's not here at all, is he?' and so on, until the creature finally stands right behind him, moving in unison, to remain hidden every time the hero spins around until the youngsters (and a good many adults) are yelling hysterically: 'He's behind you. Look out behind you!'

This kind of conversation is likely to include the other well-known exchanges: 'Oh no, he isn't!' 'Oh yes, he is!' or 'Oh no, he hasn't!' 'Oh yes, he has!' as the creature keeps disappearing from view and the actor challenges the audience, saying, for example: 'He's gone now, hasn't he?'

Active participation – on the stage

Knockabout comedy can be slapstick between the characters on the stage, which has to be very carefully timed and rehearsed to work properly. Because of their tight structure, you would be unlikely to involve the audience in these, unless the person was a 'plant'. However, a lot of fun can be had in less complicated sketches by inviting members of the audience up on the stage and involving them in the action. This might mean simply sitting them down and having the harem sing and dance to them or asking them to join in a game.

Many adults are shy of being involved – and not without good reason, for sometimes they can be made to look absolute idiots. It is wise not to go to extremes in this way in a small town or village, because word gets around and you might find yourself without volunteers at all next year – or even on the second night, if you do something too drastic, like pouring egg yolk over their heads.

Tiny tots may need a little prodding, but generally children will rush up to the stage to join in and the problem then can be fitting them all into a limited space. Present a prize for their efforts, even if only a few sweets or a silly badge, and send them back to their seats to a round of applause for being 'good sports'. Here are a few suggestions of how to involve them:

    assisting a magician or wizard
    helping the fairy make a wish come true
    giving the dame a hand – to bake a cake or hang the washing on the line
    trying to find and try on Cinderella's slipper – with lots of funny shoes and boots
    playing in an orchestra – on saucepans and bits of vacuum cleaner
    judging the Ugly Sisters beauty contest
    A variety of balloon games can be suitably adapted into appropriate games such as
       'Catching Jack's hen's golden eggs'

Active participation – off the stage

Throwing things

The audience can also be involved in the action without ever leaving their seats. Throwing things into the audience is fairly standard pantomime procedure. This might be welcome goodies like sweets (choose relatively soft ones like wine gums that will not cause injuries on impact); or a threat of something unwelcome, like a bucket of water. Have a bucket of real water and slosh it around to make the point, then at the last moment grab another bucket, full of polystyrene bits (wrap them in tinfoil first – they travel further), and throw that. The audience will think that real water is about to hurtle into the front rows.

Do not be too realistic! During one fishing scene, the cast (adults dressed up as unruly children) chucked artificial fish into the audience. I was somewhat perturbed when on the Saturday night these were irresponsibly replaced with real whiting. No one in the audience complained, because most of them fell short of the target, but sending a shower of greasy, smelly fish in their direction could have been disastrous if these had landed on a silk blouse, best suit or new hat.

Effects out front

Special effects in the hall can complement the action on stage. For example, in an eerie scene, bats and spiders on strings and pulleys can be lowered on to the heads of the audience to add to the atmosphere or balloons might cascade down from above in a celebrational scene.

Mingling with the audience

The characters can enter through the audience from the back and interact with them as they do so. They may later leave the stage action entirely and mingle with the audience – so long as a spotlight can be used to focus attention on the audience reaction. However, if not everyone can clearly see what is going on in the auditorium, it will need to be a fairly brief interlude, perhaps supported by a commentary from the stage on what is happening below. The villains might be trying to find a hiding place for their loot; the dame might be seeking a suitable partner for the ball.

Mind-reading

A mind-reading exercise can be worked into many a pantomime – asking the audience to hold up various objects in their possession to be divined by wondrous means. The wizard and his blindfolded mind-reading assistant have already rehearsed a set of incredibly obvious, corny codes for the most likely objects to be proffered. Ater a flourishing introduction about the wonders of telepathy, the wizard holds up the objects and says, for example:

'This will unlock your thoughts' – a key
'It's bound to strike you directly' – a matchstick
'I hold all your thoughts' – a bag
'Stick around and you'll get this one' – a lipstick
'I'll have to reflect on this a while – a mirror

Silly but fun!

To conclude

One way or another, the audience should feel that they are part of the pantomime. It is not something just for the players to create in isolation. What happens up on stage can never be a separate entity; its impact, even in straight theatre, depends on the audience response.

In pantomime there is the best excuse in the world to make the action tangible by directly involving the audience. It is important for the survival of live theatre that the production makes the most of the opportunities that live performance offers as opposed to film or television. Give the audience a chance to contribute in all sorts of different ways. Throughout, they should feel that they are welcome to join in – to sing, shout, cheer and comment – and that they are a vital element, even part of the story at times. Then crossing that barrier of the proscenium arch will be a stimulating and very enjoyable experience – for audience and actors alike.

9

Publicity and printed matter

Enormous energies are ploughed into the production of a pantomime. The rehearsals can be great fun. Often, watching the buffoons within the group creating havoc with my script I reflect, as tears of hysterical laughter stream away the remnants of my mascara down my face, that it is the camaraderie of rehearsals that makes everything worthwhile, as much as the shows themselves.

None the less, we should all be bitterly disappointed if no one turned up to watch us perform. Enthusiasm must also be invested into the publicity of the production to ensure full houses and a healthy budget for the society.

Start early

It is important to start early, especially to prepare the printed matter. No matter how often you do it, somehow this always takes considerably more time to put together than is ever anticipated. Especially if you are using an outside printer, reasonable notice and time to check everything will be required.

Most societies today include somebody who has access to a typewriter, word processor, or desktop publishing system of some kind, as well as photocopying services, so that programmes, posters, tickets and press releases can be created in house. This simplifies life and reduces costs. However, if the computer is in the office rather than the home, this may mean the willing contributor working through lunch breaks or persuading someone else to help outside normal working hours, so it is still important to make sure all the material is gathered together as soon as possible.

Programmes always have to be finalised at the last minute because there are bound to be some changes and/or additions, but there is no reason why the basic information and structure cannot be brought together quite early to avoid panic during the last week.

A longer publicity campaign can help to build up interest locally and means more notice can be given to the press if you wish them to attend the show or to provide pre-production publicity.

The publicity manager

If one member of the group is in charge of publicity regularly, contact with local newspapers and radio stations can be built up and form a firm foundation for succeeding advertising campaigns. Even just ferreting out all the names and telephone numbers takes time and it is very wasteful if this information disappears between productions, so, whether the role is swapped or not, do keep a clean, updated copy of the contact list on file for future use.

The main qualities of the good publicity manager are enthusiasm and persistence, tempered by charm. It may take several telephone calls and letters to achieve the required result but once you are through to the person in charge, make sure you positively bubble with the fun of the production. A letter can convey the information in an accessible manner if the main points are listed and starred rather than lost in vast paragraphs.

HUMPTY DUMPTY COMES TO TOWN!
* Entertainment for all the family in Toyland!
* Exciting transformation scenes will fly you to the moon and transport you to the bottom of the sea.
* Songs and dance in abundance!
* Masses of laughs – especially with Dame Egg!
* Tickets nearly sold out. Book yours now!
* Wednesday 5 to Saturday 8 January in the Town Hall. 7.30 p.m.

Press and radio

A publicity manager who is already actively involved in the production will have a good base of information to begin the campaign, but he or she may still find it useful to talk closely with the producer and scriptwriter to tease out interesting snippets to capture the imagination of both the journalists and potential audiences.

Make sure the information comes across in a lively way. Headlines like LOCAL GROUP REHEARSE LATEST PANTO with a factual account of the play dates and times are all well and good; more compelling is a headline that reads LOCAL GIANT COMPLAINS OF HICCUPS! and goes on to explain that Jack's giant in the latest production says that eating up Nurseryland characters and then dancing on the stage is giving him indigestion. Make sure the giant remembers to mention the performance dates and so on. Local papers are usually happy to publish handouts of information of this kind, especially if accompanied by a photograph or two. This may mean chivvying the costume department to provide one or two advance costumes.

Towns and villages often publish a 'What's On' pamphlet available in libraries or shops. Make sure your pantomime is included. Try to persuade the press and local radio and television channels to give advance publicity at least one week before rather than a piece appearing halfway through the production run or even after it has finished. A good write-up afterwards is a nice boost for the society but it won't sell any tickets.

Capitalise on previous productions

When a society has built up a reputation for good productions, this is the best lever with which to prise folk out of their armchairs and into the local village hall. Those who already believe in you are the backbone of the audience, and yield greater returns than any other form of advertising.

It is more difficult, therefore, for a first-time production to pull in vast numbers.

The society may want to limit the number of performances accordingly to ensure reasonably full houses rather than half-empty ones and let the numbers of evenings gradually increase along with its reputation. Do not lose this impetus. Individual members should all keep lists of their friends and relatives and colleagues who have been before and contact these people each time to remind them how much they enjoyed it last year. The society secretary or ticket-sales rep should send out advance information and booking forms to everyone in the group and perhaps to regular supporters as well.

If the production is as good as ever, there will be no trouble maintaining audiences. A hard core of solid support can gradually be added to as new members join and bring fresh contacts along as new audience members.

Never be complacent, however. Audiences need constant encouragement and it is a mistake to assume that everyone will turn up as usual, particularly for the midweek performances.

Keep up the standards and, as the word spreads about how good the productions are, the circle of audience will sweep yet wider.

Selling tickets

A half-hearted approach to selling tickets will never work. Constantly maintain that bubbling enthusiasm and encourage people to come in families and groups. Try offering special incentives, such as a family night with reduced rates for four members of the family or more.

Contact other local societies and agree to visit each other's shows as party bookings on a reciprocal basis. We can learn a lot and have great evenings out by sharing amateur theatre in this way. You can also advertise in drama association magazines which link local groups' news together from your county or town.

Contact the schools. Someone reliable with small children to collect from school can be a useful contact. A 'colour in the poster' competition in the school will be a useful reminder of the show if the teaching staff or the local shops are willing to distribute these.

Give members goals to aim for (perhaps with silly medals or little prizes) for such achievements as:

selling the most tickets
selling tickets to six people who have never been to any of your productions before
persuading Major and Mrs Hacket to come
selling to a group of more than eight people
having more than ten relatives willing to come

One of the problems with aggressive ticket selling is extracting the money from advance sales. It can be difficult to persuade people to part with money if you do not have the actual tickets to hand over. At the same time, many societies impose strict rules regarding this so that members are not handed over the real tickets until payment has been received.

This can discourage members from selling so it is often advisable to allow a limited number of tickets to be given out to members on a sale or return basis at the first stage of selling. This might exclude Saturday night tickets, which generally sell out very quickly anyway.

Generally, if people have actually handed over hard cash they are more likely to turn up than if they agree to pay on the door or settle up with friends later. There is always a member of the group being left high and dry by friends who do not bother to come, unaware that the member has had to part with his or her own money to purchase the tickets for them.

Timing is important. Advance booking should be made available to members of the society for a limited period with a deadline for the receipt of monies before the tickets go public.

However the sales are handled, the ticket-sales operative (who may be the publicity manager or part of the front-of-house team or the treasurer or somebody totally independent) will need to keep close tabs on who has received advance tickets and on the exchange of monies for these.

Local shops can generally be persuaded to sell tickets. Do help them by providing clear information about dates and prices and a safe container for the cash. And, in the politest possible way, try to make sure that all the members of the staff are aware of the ticket-sales system so that no prospective audience members are turned away because 'Sheila's off today and I don't know anything about it. Can you come back tomorrow?'

Local charity organisations will often be pleased to offer your tickets to pensioners or other such deserving groups and may be willing to make a block booking with you.

The main factor in selling of any kind is to be positive and enthusiastic, to make people feel that they will really be missing a treat if they do not come along and to present the vital information clearly.

Posters

If the society has kept in touch with its established support, posters will remind this regular audience of dates and times. If they have not yet purchased tickets through members of the group or a direct-mail onslaught, the posters will remind them to buy their tickets now.

Posters also serve to draw in some new audience, perhaps people who have recently moved into the area or who are visiting or who feel it is about time they sampled the efforts of their local group. And children may persuade their parents to take them if the poster is sufficiently bright and eye-catching.

Local shops, schools, garages, pubs and libraries are generally willing to display these posters.

They tend to be happiest accepting A4-size posters rather than huge ones which take up too much window or noticeboard space.

The poster can also be reduced to A5 size and used as a flyer. Run off lots of these so that they can be left in the local shops, pubs and libraries for people to take home with them. The local newsagent might even be persuaded to pop them in the newspapers or they can be posted through doors by members (or members' children) and stuck to members' car windows to spread the word yet further afield.

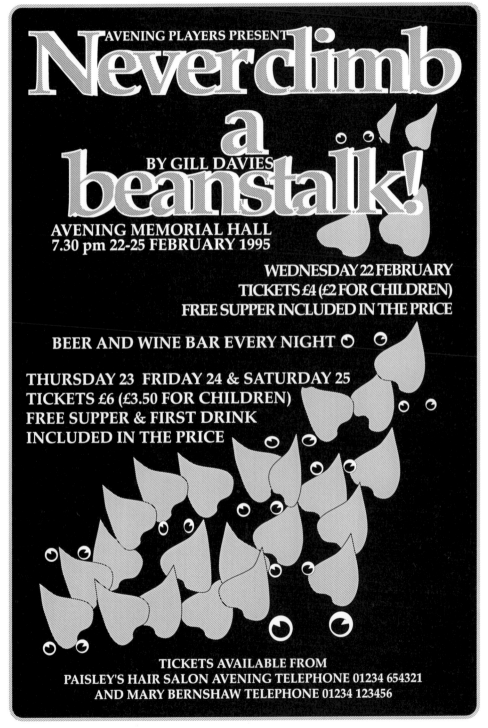

An example of a poster which conveys all the vital information.

What should the posters say?

The essential facts to include are the following:

the name of the group;
the pantomime title;
author (this is generally a requirement of the granting of licence or copyright);
the venue; the days;
dates *and* time of performances;
the source(s) of tickets (names and telephone numbers if possible);
entrance price and any reductions available.

Make it easy for people to understand all this information and easy to obtain tickets. If the poster is illegible or it is a struggle to find out just who is selling tickets, or if the single source is always out or shut, many potential purchasers will be lost through their frustration.

It goes without saying but I'll say it! The poster should look good. A scrappy scribbled tatty piece of paper will not reflect well on the group. Ensure the poster is attractive, well laid out and legible, and, if the weather reduces externally displayed posters to wet rags, replace these with fresh ones on a regular basis. Update the information. Slashes across saying ONLY 10 SATURDAY SEATS NOW LEFT or HURRY! HURRY! NEARLY SOLD OUT! may encourage those who have been thinking about buying tickets but have not yet committed themselves.

Attract the eye

Colour is important. The printing can be black or white but if so, make sure the posters are on a coloured stock of paper. Alternatively, areas can be filled in with bright felt-tip colours.

Pictorial elements are fun. Sketches, cartoons or computer-generated images will attract the eye if they are well done, but much depends on the talents available. Bad drawing looks unprofessional and is best avoided if in doubt. Ask around within your group and their contacts to find out who has artistic talents or is good at lettering and handling typography. There may, for example, be a cartoonist in your midst who can depict the actual members of the society in a humorous way or someone skilled in the drawing program on their Apple Mac who can provide black-and-white and a few colour versions of an exciting poster.

Someone might be good at writing lively copy lines to capture the imagination of the passers by.

An overall style: posters, tickets and programmes

The style of the poster should reflect the style of the production. The general design, the lettering or typeface and any drawing or imagery should be used consistently in all the printed matter. The way the information is presented and the approach (humourous or medieval, for example) should help to convey the feel of this particular production. Moreover, do try to retain an integrated approach to posters, programmes and tickets.

Tickets and programmes

Print these too on a decent weight of paper so that they do not look shoddy as soon as they are handled or blow away in the first puff of air. As suggested with

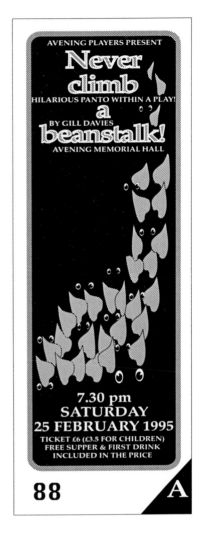

Example of a related programme and ticket. The 'A' on the right stands for Adult and can be cut off if the ticket is used for a child. Numbers (bottom left) can be stamped on to help keep track of ticket sales or to indicate seat numbers.

Do remember to keep copies of all your printed and publicity material, as well as photographs and press cuttings. They will create an invaluable archive for future reference.

the posters, draw on local talent and resources, reflect the overall style of the pantomime and ensure that all the different elements of printed matter clearly belong to the same integrated production.

Tickets

The tickets can be a reduced version of the poster, with a few modifications. This saves time, especially if these are being computer generated. Omit the source of tickets but include the following:

the name of the group
the pantomime title
the venue
time of performance.

Then there are the variables:

the single date for which ticket is applicable
seat number if applicable
reduction if applicable.

Print the tickets on a different colour for each night for greater clarity. This helps enormously when selling. And make sure the day as well as the date appears so no one turns up on Friday instead of Thursday because they have got the date wrong.

A tear-off corner can be used to indicate a child or pensioner reduction. Seat numbers need not be pre-printed – this would be costly – but some sort of numbering is essential to keep track of the number of tickets sold. Special machines can be purchased which automatically roll on the numbers as you stamp the backs of the tickets. These might be used as seat numbers, depending on the booking system of individual societies. The advantages of pre-booking seats are that it is an excellent incentive to audiences to book early; audiences do not need to arrive so soon to grab the best seats; and friends can be sure they will sit together if they book early enough. The disadvantage is that it takes extra planning and organisation by members and ticket-sale helpers. But generally it is worth the effort.

Programme content

Make the programmes fun to read, not a boring after-thought. Include a lively introduction by the producer, the author and/or the leader of the group, conveying the ethos of the production and the society, with some titbits of information about what has happened during rehearsals and plans for future productions.

Make the programme start to sell the show right away, awakening the audience's interest with intriguing comments and lead-ins to the evening's entertainment. Welcome them to the evening, invite them to join in and draw them into the story or the setting. Coax them into the right frame of mind from the word go with intriguing snippets of information about the play, the characters, the setting and the story. The programme should include:

A cover with the play title, author and dates, including the year. Very useful later when trying to remember what you did when!

Introduction to whet the appetite of the audience, set the scene and encourage them to feel part of the show.

List of acts and scenes Make it clear when intervals occur and the duration of these and when refreshments are available.

The cast list, which may include the producer and the musicians.

The backstage team list

Other credits In these acknowledgements and thanks for help, it is important to remember everyone and make sure official gratitude is expressed for loan of furniture, seating, sale of tickets and so on.

Internal advertising Invitations to join the group, hire costumes, buy T-shirts, have photograph taken with the dragon, become a 'friend' or patron, buy bottles of wine and so on. Include names and addresses of contacts within the society for future reference.

External advertising for local trade, if applicable.

Coming soon Information on future productions.

Advertising

Use the programme as a vehicle to attract new members: include all the relevant names and telephone numbers to contact. If there are any other facilities on offer – such as society T-shirts or costume hire – do not miss this opportunity to advertise.

Some societies ask local businesses to advertise in the programmes, and this can be an excellent source of income. It should be appreciated fully, however, that attracting and keeping advertisers, as well as billing and collecting the monies due, takes a good deal of organisation. One or two members will need to undertake this aspect specifically and devote their energies to this end well before the time of the production.

Attracting advertisements is another reason for aiming at a good-quality programme that is not instantly thrown away. It will be easier to invite local traders to advertise in something relatively substantial and collectable. The revenue does help cover the costs.

Sometimes societies are lucky enough to attract sponsorship from local business and this should not be overlooked as a further possible source of income.

Numbers of programmes

Some people never buy programmes and most couples and families share one between them. As a rough guide, reckon on one in three of your audience purchasing a programme.

However, do not forget that they are a memento for the participants. Allow one each for all those actively involved in the production front and backstage. It is especially welcome if these can be presented to the cast and backstage team before they go on sale so that they feel they have an advance copy rather than having to grab an audience leftover.

The number of programmes sold can be boosted if they are numbered, or have a raffle ticket attached, so that the lucky-number programme can be announced later and a prize awarded.

Proof stage

Do try to run off a rough copy of the programme about one week ahead so that this can be passed around the members to check. Somebody may have been omitted or a name spelled wrong or not as the person likes (for example, Katherine may prefer to be called Kathy). It is advisable to allow opportunity for several pairs of eyes to check the programme before it is reproduced in large quantities.

Other publicity

A good publicity campaign needs to start early, and to be positive and enthusiastic. Follow the first thrust with an equally energetic, well-structured advertising campaign to reap extra audience and remind stalwart supporters to come along.

As a final reminder that the pantomime is taking place, it is worth considering a procession through the streets in costume – perhaps on the weekend before the production. Suitably clad players (and/or their children) can seize this opportunity to hand out flyers and arouse local interest in the production. It takes courage and enthusiasm but once under way, especially if the weather is kind, it can be quite stimulating and provides players with a taste of street theatre.

A banner over the hall will give the final flourish to this advertising campaign and will remind all the local supporters that the play is imminent. It also give an additional boost to the anticipation of an eventful evening when people arrive, especially if it can be lit.

One of the most effective forms of local advertising is to hang a banner on the venue. Further banners can be placed in other conspicuous places nearby – but do ask permission first.

10

Children – on and off the stage

It is worth remembering that many adults are still only children at heart and much of what applies to children will be applicable to them as well. In fact, pantomimes are only ostensibly performed for children. In many cases, it would be true to say that the adults who perform are really only using the children as an excuse for them to indulge in the fun that putting on a pantomime allows.

However, it is certainly true that a large number of the audience will be very young and the entertainment must keep them well amused. Bored, restless youngsters create a lot of noise and distraction and it can be very difficult to give a good performance if little ones are crying and running about. So it really is important that every member of the audience thoroughly enjoys the show, whatever their age.

Generally, what works for children, if it is done well, will work for adults too. By the same token, if the pantomime is heavy-weight and tedious, adults will be just as bored – although they may be slightly more polite. They may not get up and run around or throw a wobbly in the centre aisle but they will shuffle in their seats, yawn, exchange pained glances – and never come again.

We expect theatre to cater for a much wider age range than any book or game. Obviously, from, say, three years old to ninety-three, there are vastly different levels of humour, taste, knowledge and understanding, but so long as no one theme or factor dominates for too long and there is something for everyone happening – if not concurrently, at least in fast succession – it is possible to strike a happy balance.

Children in the audience

Maintaining interest is vital. Keep the changes rolling, let the children join in and participate as often as possible, both by shouting and singing in the auditorium and by coming up on the stage, and provide little surprises and unexpected twists, turns and events. Try to achieve the following and you will keep *all* age groups absorbed.

Momentum

Do not overstretch any one scene. Make sure that the pace does not slow down. If you are conscious in rehearsal that a particular scene is not really working and that you see it as something to be tolerated for the sake of the plot, think again. Can it be changed or cut? What is wrong? Make sure every scene is up to scratch. Avoid overlong soliloquies and songs; avoid people standing still for long periods.

Constant change

Lots of change is stimulating and will make the show lively. Keep the scenes short and snappy with plenty of variety and try to include at least one or two really exciting changes of scenery and costume. If there is always something different and new happening, there will be constant stimulation and interest. No one will have time to be bored.

Story line

It is tempting in pantomime to go off at tangents so as to include lots of different elements. This is fine to a degree but do make sure that the plot is not lost entirely. It can be difficult for small children to follow what is happening if there are too many illogical excursions. Try to weave all the various elements neatly into the plot.

Do not take the story line for granted. Make sure it is clear. Just because all of you know exactly what happens to Cinderella, it can be easy to forget that for the wide-eyed wee tot in the front row, this story happens to be entirely new – a first-time experience.

Visual humour and effects

No matter how good the plot, dialogue and music, the pantomime needs to excite the eyes, to provide lots to see and watch. Visual humour and magical effects, colour and costume, lights and dramatic scenery appeal to all age groups but are especially important in the captivation of children. And if you do get the visual elements right, children will be greatly impressed and be carried along by the magic far more than the adults. They will remember and talk about the show for a long, long time. It may, indeed, be their only experience of live theatre, so try to make it really special for them.

Include a variety of visual stimuli – whatever suits the plot. Since you may wish to do shows annually you cannot use every trick every year but there are many possibilities and variations. Pantomimes can include, for example, the following:

slapstick comedy scenes
dance sequences
transformation scenes
magic and conjuring tricks or effects
lighting and special effects (such as strange eyes shining in a dark forest, snowflakes
    falling, coloured smoke, flashes of light when the genie appears, strobe lighting)
puppet shows
masks
projection of film or slides
shadow plays – large and small-scale
boisterous action: chases, fights, hide and seek, tumbling and falling over – and acrobatics,
    if you have space
animal characters

Contrast

To heighten the dramatic effect and to maintain interest, any play should have light and shade, build up to a climax and have lots of contrasting characters, scenes and deliveries. Pantomime is no exception. In fact, the stories are full of opposites – good and evil being paramount. For example, bear in mind these few opposites from the great store of possibilities. They may seem obvious but it is easy to overlook the obvious. Play opposites against each other to great effect, whether in characters, physique of actors, the interpretation of lines, feeling and mood, tangible scenery or staging – whatever is appropriate.

> good and evil
> noise and quiet
> bright light and dark
> happy and sad
> bravery and cowardice
> fast and slow
> clever and silly
> big and little
> old and young

Children on stage

'Never act with children and animals!' This well-known saying flies around the dressing rooms every year in almost every pantomime production where children are participating. It can be provoked by two totally different aspects of children's involvement. The most general use refers to the way in which children can all too easily steal the scene from the adult actors, intentionally or otherwise. The other reason is the havoc they can cause backstage if given half a chance to run riot.

If children are going to be in the play, a good deal of extra organisation is inevitably involved. In the long term this will pay dividends for all the society's productions: even the youngest actors do grow up and it is wonderful to have young people learning theatre skills within the group.

Moreover, youngsters are great fun to have around and the exuberance that can be difficult to manage in a crowded dressing room is a great asset in rehearsals and on the stage. To share in their enthusiasm is very rewarding.

Here are the factors to consider when deciding whether to involve youngsters in this year's show.

The plus factors

Energy Children are enthusiastic. They bubble over with energy, which is marvellous up on stage. It can be a tonic to be surrounded by a keen group of youngsters after dealing with sometimes jaded or complaining adults.

Children learn fast They absorb lines very quickly – often everybody else's as well as their own. There are exceptions, of course, but on the whole, children have impressively keen memories and are very adaptable. Children are also very direct. In general, they will be far more forthcoming about their wishes and talents than adults, so there is far less beating about the bush.

Audiences love them! A well-disciplined, well-rehearsed group of children will add a whole new dimension to the acting, singing and dancing. And if things do go wrong, the audience is very forgiving and warm towards youngsters. Moreover, the tiniest are guaranteed to capture the audience's heart.

Swelling the audience You will be guaranteed larger audiences – all the relatives quickly demand tickets.

New members Children provide a source of new membership – not just the children themselves, who can grow up with the society, but also their relatives, who may join the front or backstage teams. Their families may be relatively young themselves.

A good mix It is good for the society to have a cross-section of age groups who can all learn from each other: it widens the horizons. Theatre breaks down all sorts of barriers, including the generation gap.

Family membership Some adult actors enjoy including their children and sharing their love of amateur dramatics with the rest of the family. Having their offspring involved in the occasional production may make life easier if both partners are active members.

The minus factors – and how to solve them

Firm control is needed Children can be noisy and wild, especially when they are excited, and left to their own devices, will quickly turn the rehearsal hall into a playground. Even worse mayhem will break out backstage during performances if they are not properly controlled. First night nerves will make the adults snappy and less tolerant of excited, boisterous children and, anyway, calm quiet is *essential* backstage.

Make sure discipline is firm right from the beginning, that the children's abilities are fully explored and stretched and that they are always kept very busy.

Extra personnel will be needed to organise the children during gaps in rehearsals and performances to keep them happy and quiet so they do not disturb everyone else or interfere with the smooth running of the production in any way.

Space problems Many dressing rooms in amateur theatres are mixed, with adults of both sexes in various states of undress. In any case, children will need separate space. More room may be needed to accommodate the children during performances than the hall can readily offer. If this is the situation, see if they can be stationed in a nearby house watching a video, perhaps, and runners sent to collect them when their entrances are due. Make sure the baby-sitters are responsible. My son was taught to play poker and gamble when appearing in *Under Milkwood* at a tender age.

Extra rehearsals Rehearsals will have to be arranged to suit the earlier hours children can be out. These may initially be entirely separate rehearsals, perhaps run by someone other than the producer in the early stages – and they may stay that way until the dress rehearsals if the scene or sequence is entirely independent.

If there is a separate producer, the overall producer will have to drop into the rehearsals at regular intervals to ensure everything is running smoothly and integrates well into the rest of the show.

When the children interact with adult actors, obviously they need to rehearse together too. So, once the basics have been grasped, the timing of rehearsals will need to be fixed so that early in the evening, the adult actors required in the children's scenes are all there to do the children's bits. Do not forget to find a suitable time to practise the finale and final bow. It is no good suddenly remembering the night before the show that there are a mass of extra bodies to accommodate and expecting the children to know exactly what to do if they have never been given a chance to rehearse this properly.

Final thoughts

Producing and acting with youngsters can be enormous fun. Much depends on how well disciplined they are and how supportive the parents can be in helping to provide transport, baby-sitting and bringing and collecting them promptly at rehearsals.

Some societies find it keeps everybody happy if children are involved in alternate productions; others give the children the opportunity to put on entirely separate shows.

It is up to individual groups and to the producers concerned. Do not take on children half-heartedly, for they will place taxing demands on time, energy and human resources, but, as with every other aspect of creative work, the greater the effort, the greater the rewards.

Children enjoy being involved in a pantomime. They always appeal to audiences and their inclusion has the added bonus of helping to swell ticket sales – as usually all the families will want to see their younger members perform!

11

Stock characters and story lines

Everyone who comes to a pantomime, except perhaps the very youngest child, arrives anticipating certain familiar ingredients. The children look forward to the fairy tale contrast of good and evil characters, to fairies and demons, witches and sweet princesses, to the burlesque antics of the dame and clowns. The adults enjoy the nostalgia and sharing with their children at least one or two threads from their own memories of childhood family entertainment. The familiarity is comfortable; it is part of Christmas past and the ongoing traditions that make that season so special.

Because today so much has radically changed, especially in the world of entertainment, often a pantomime visit is the only taste of live drama that the family share, so its stable qualities are especially welcome.

Traditional pantomime characters

It is fun to give the audience a few surprises, of course, and to adapt and build upon the stock characters, but especially if you are writing your own script, it may be useful to analyse their basic elements.

Dame

A comic female character played by a man. Often the role is that of the hero's mother. Dames include:

Dame Twankey in *Aladdin*
Mother Goose
the Cook in *Dick Whittington*
the Ugly Sisters in *Cinderella*
Mrs Crusoe in *Robinson Crusoe*
Mother Hubbard or Dame Trot in *Jack and the Beanstalk*
the Queen of Hearts in several stories, including *Puss in Boots* and *Alice in Wonderland*.

The character is generally over the top. Jack Trip (probably today's best known and most experienced dame) says that she should be clearly seen as 'a nice man being a nice lady' whom children can like and relate to and laugh with comfortably. The dame is the focus of the pantomime's humour and burlesque elements and will be involved in slapstick scenes and much audience participation and the occasional touch of pathos.

The dame is an essential ingredient of pantomime.

False boobs are optional. And high heels are best avoided – they impede the knockabout antics. Anyway, the dame should in no way resemble a drag artist; dainty boots or crazy Doc Marten's are best. She often does a comic striptease routine, revealing about twenty layers of bloomers, numerous hot-water bottles strapped around her waist, vast corsets and vivid striped socks.

Keep her light, frothy and fun, warm and motherly but still obviously masculine.

Principal boy

Generally played by an actress with good legs to reveal, this character is the hero of the story and has been played by women since the mid-nineteenth century. In the 1960s and 1970s, male pop stars and well-known comedians often assumed these roles in professional productions, but in amateur theatre, the parts are still generally taken by tallish females with a good figure.

He is thigh-slapping, jaunty, chivalrous, brave and in love with the heroine. He comes to her rescue and fights off numerous baddies. He often sings love duets with the heroine, but these can be excruciatingly boring for young children and should be kept fairly brief. Typical principal boys include:

Dick Whittington
Robin Hood
Aladdin
Jack (the giant-killer)
Prince Charming.

Traditionally the principal boy speaks the last two lines of the pantomime but only does so in actual performances – not during rehearsals – to avoid bad luck!

The heroine (principal girl)

Ideally, she should be youthful and pretty, willing to sing, and able to act a sweet, innocent character without seeming too twee. She must be charming and appealing and have the audience totally on her side. Heroines are sometimes princesses – or become princesses by the end of the story. Typical heroines include:
Little Red Riding Hood
Princess Badroubaldour in *Aladdin*
Cinderella
Beauty in *Beauty and the Beast*
Maid Marion in *Babes in the Wood*
Sleeping Beauty.

Goodies

As well as the hero and heroine, the goodies can include the traditional pantomime good fairy. She wears a glittering costume, wings and coronet and waves a magic wand in her right hand to help the hero and heroine through their adventures and in her left hand to curse the baddies. She can be young but is not necessarily so.

Alternatively, the fairy can be less obvious and without the sparkle when she appears as a fairy godmother or an old lady gathering wood in the forest, or perhaps as a gypsy who turns the tide of fortune for the hero and heroine.

Whatever her exact role in the story, this character is the embodiment of good and always appears stage right.

She is often lit by a pink spotlight. Some fairies, like Tinkerbell in *Peter Pan*, invite or need the audience to help them along in various ways, thus encouraging audience participation. Their magic is generally the pivot of the pantomime's transformation scenes.

Baddies

Baddies, the embodiment of evil, appear stage left and are generally lit by a green spotlight, although fiery red is occasionally used. Their aim is to seize the princess or the treasure, magic or wealth that they believe might make the heroine more accessible. Baddies are constantly thwarted by the hero and the fairy or other goodies!

In swirling cloak and evil mask or make-up, the main baddie appears fairly early on to explain his or her evil intents. The audience should be encouraged to boo and hiss these nasty pieces of work. The baddie should try, however, not to overfrighten the very youngest members of the audience. Typical baddies include:
the demon king in several story lines, including *Mother Goose*
King Rat in *Dick Whittington*
the wolf in *Little Red Riding Hood*
the queen in *Snow White*
Uncle Abanazar in *Aladdin*
the witch in *Hansel and Gretel*
the sorcerer in *Sinbad the Sailor*.

Clowns

The term 'clown' is used here to describe any funny characters who add to the buffoonery and knockabout comic elements of pantomime. There might indeed be circus-like clowns in the story; certainly there are circus-like elements involved in the slapstick – the comics may well end up with trousers full of water or covered in paint or pastry. The most famous clown of all, Joe Grimaldi, never appeared in the circus ring at all but only in theatre.

Often a bad character, like the Sheriff of Nottingham in *Robin Hood*, will employ riotously inept accomplice villains or bailiffs who are veritable clowns, stuffing sausages down their clothing, tripping over their feet, bumping into each other and hurling custard pies around. The Ugly Sisters can sometimes slide into the clown roles as well. These are comedy double acts.

Alternatively, the clown may be a solitary comedian, like Wishee Washee in *Aladdin*, or perhaps a Simple Simon character who wants to help the heroine but who also carries the pantomime humour and gets the audience on his side – as Buttons does in *Cinderella*.

See pages 75-8 for further information on comedy techniques.

Animal roles

Animal characters add a lot of fun to a pantomime and can be appealing or comic or both. Children in the audience love them and many actors enjoy the challenge of being a frog or cat, a goose, a horse, a camel or cow – although the back ends, when required, may be less desirable roles.

The imagination to take on animal characteristics and being able to achieve a good rapport with the audience are the main qualities required. Agility and suppleness are useful and often the animal has to sing and dance. Voice and movement, suitable expressions and detailed observation of the specific animal's behaviour will all help the actor to portray an animal convincingly.

The pantomime cow – in rehearsal.

The pantomime cow – in performance.

If there are no obvious animal characters in the story, it may be worth introducing one. I added a parrot as a go-between spying for Captain Hook and Long John Silver in a crazy mixed-up pirate pantomime called *Treasure Spyland* and a dragon into a Robin Hood story; both characters added enormously to the rollicking fun of the productions.

Generally the animals are loving friends of the hero or heroine and include:

Jack's cow, usually called Daisy, in *Jack and the Beanstalk*
Puss in Boots
Dick Whittington's cat
all the animals in *Toad of Toad Hall*
the goose in *Mother Goose*
the lion in *The Wizard of Oz*.

Parental roles and figures of authority

There are numerous kings and queens and parent characters in pantomime. These include fathers like Baron Hardup in *Cinderella* and Alderman Fitzwarren in *Dick Whittington*, wicked stepmothers (in *Cinderella* and *Snow White*), Emperors (in *Aladdin* and *The Emperor's Nightingale*), the queens in *Alice in Wonderland*, and Old King Cole in various nursery-rhyme based stories.

These older characters are often the enemies of the heroine. As such, they will need to be overcome by the hero's bravery. Alternatively, they may be the parents of the heroine and will need to be won over by the hero's charm – and, generally, through his acquisition of wealth and position. Usually they are good strong characters and offer rewarding roles to older members of the society.

Pantomime & date first performed	Heroes & Principal boys	Heroines	Goodies	Baddies	Dames	Animals	Parents/figures of authority
Aladdin Boxing Day 1788	Aladdin	Princess Badroubaldour	Genie	Uncle Abanazar	Widow Twankey	Camel in Egypt	Emperor
Ali Baba & the 40 Thieves 1846	Ali Baba's son	Morgiana*	Morgiana*	Wicked robbers	Morgiana, Ali Baba's servant*	Mule	Ali's brother, Kasim, & wife
Babes in the Wood 1793	Robin Hood Children	Maid Marian	Woodland Fairy Cock Robin	Wicked Baron Uncle & murderers; Sheriff of Nottingham			
Cinderella 1804	Prince Charming	Cinderella	Fairy Godmother Buttons	Wicked Stepmother Ugly Sisters	The Ugly Sisters	(sometimes) Cat and mice	Baron Hardup
Dick Whittington 1814	Dick Whittington	Alice Fitzwarren	Fairy of the bells	King Rat	The cook	Dick's Cat Rats	Alderman Fitzwarren Sultan of Morocco
Jack and the Beanstalk 1819	Jack		Fairy (disguised as old lady?)	Giant Blunderbore	Mother Hubbard or Dame Trot	Cow (usually called Daisy)	Bean seller
Little Red Riding Hood 1803	Woodcutter	Little Red Riding Hood	Forest Fairy	Demon Wolf	Grandma		Squire
Mother Goose 1806 or before	Colin (Mother Goose's son)		(sometimes) Good Fairy	Demon King Discontent Bailiffs	Mother Goose	Goose (Priscilla)	Squire
Puss in Boots early 1800's	Miller's son	Princess	Fairy Grimalkin	Ogre	(sometimes) Queen of Hearts	Puss in Boots (spell-bound prince)	
Robinson Crusoe 1871	Robinson Crusoe	Native Princess Polly Perkins	Man Friday	Pirate King Cannibal Queen	Mrs Crusoe	Dog, Cat, Goat & Parrot	
Sleeping Beauty 1822	Brave Prince	Princess	Good Fairy	Wicked Fairy	Queen*		King and Queen*
Snow White popular 1950s	Handsome Prince	Snow White	The Seven Dwarfs	Queen (Wicked Stepmother)			Snow White's father

*interchangeable in different versions

Stock characters: many of the most popular pantomimes today were first performed in the early 1800s. It is interesting to note that no pantomime horse seems to exist! Asterisks indicate when a particular character can be portrayed variously in different versions of the story.

Story lines

A visit to the children's section of the local library might provide inspiration and will help to fill in the details of the stories for those who are writing their own versions. The list that follows covers most of the pantomimes already performed and available as scripts (there may be several versions), subject to the usual licensing and copyright restrictions.

Classic folk and fairy tales, and the best known pantomimes:

Jack and the Beanstalk
Dick Whittington
Aladdin
Puss in Boots
Cinderella
The Sleeping Beauty
Snow White and the Seven Dwarfs
Little Red Riding Hood
Ali Baba and the Forty Thieves
Goldilocks and the Three Bears
Robinson Crusoe
Babes in the Wood (a Victorian concoction based on an old English ballad in which Robin Hood and Maid Marion rescue two small children sent to be murdered in the woods by their wicked baron uncle)

Also

Sinbad the Sailor
The Snow Queen
Hansel and Gretel
Beauty and the Beast
The Frog Prince
The Tinder Box
Rumpelstiltskin
Hop o' My Thumb
The Emperor's Singing Nightingale
Jack the Giant Killer

Pantomimes based on nursery rhymes

Old King Cole
Humpty Dumpty
Mother Goose
The Queen of Hearts
Little Jack Horner
Little Bo Peep
Tom, the Piper's son
Old Mother Hubbard
Jack and Jill
The House that Jack Built

Children's productions

Other stories regularly produced for children at Christmas and New Year include:

Peter Pan
Pinocchio
Tom Thumb
Treasure Island
A Christmas Carol
Alice in Wonderland
Alice through the Looking Glass
The Lion, the Witch and the Wardrobe
The Wizard of Oz
A Thousand and One Arabian Nights
The Wind in the Willows
Toad of Toad Hall
Beatrix Potter stories

12

The opening night and aftermath

Opening Night

Nerves

It is important that the cast feel happy and excited, ready to start with enthusiasm. Although there will be a few inevitable first-night nerves, the exhilaration of receiving an audience response at last will soon overcome these, so long as all the cast have rehearsed thoroughly, have learned their lines well in advance and know that they can rely on each other and the support of a good backstage team. Then the butterflies in the stomach will soon disappear, leaving an edge of excitement that can make for a really fine performance.

There is no excuse for a poor first-night show. There may indeed be the odd technical hiccup with a new or untried piece of equipment whose contrariness slipped through the net in the technical run-through, but the well-rehearsed group should take any minor mishaps in their stride. And if the odd line is lost through first-night stage fright, this will not matter a jot so long as the pace is maintained.

A last-minute read-through of the lines can help to alleviate first-night nerves.

Dissuade the cast from hovering in the wings to watch, tripping up stage hands and generally getting in the way. An intercom to the dressing room so that the cast can hear the play will help enormously. (If a camera can be set out front and linked to a mnitor backstage, this is even better.) No one has an excuse for missing their cue.

Peering through the curtains to see if Mum or Aunty Freda has turned up should also be frowned upon. It looks awful out front, and if one person starts, everybody will join in. It is irresistible once someone has succumbed and there will soon be a heaving mass of bodies, giggling and scrambling for a viewpoint.

Awareness of relatives out front, especially husbands, wives, boyfriends and girlfriends, can add to the tension and there may be a resurrection of the first-night nerves for individual performers later in the week, when this occurs. Others rise to the occasion and revel in the opportunity to show off to somebody they know out front. So, if there is any unexpected change in the level of a performance, it may be that a relative is to blame.

Concentrate on what is happening, both on and offstage. Relax too much in the changing room, sharing a joke and a glass of beer, and you forget how soon your entrance is due. The pace is always different with an audience, and there is always the risk that the cast may skip a few lines or pages, and gobble up the gap you thought you had.

Drinking to calm the nerves can have a dire effect. The adrenaline will be flowing well already and most people feel on a real high after a successful opening night, without any alcohol to boost the glow of triumph. A good first performance is very exciting *and* can be achieved best by a relatively sober cast.

Team spirit

Just how the team pull together and support each other is very important. By team, I mean both actors and the backstage workers, whose vital contributions are now being put to the test too, along with the acting and production elements. Indeed, the actors' performances depend on the support of the backstage team, who will be feeling nervous and excited just like those out front.

Basically, on and off the stage, if everyone considers everyone else's feelings and needs as unselfishly as possible and rallies to the cause of making the show work well, the pantomime will benefit greatly. Help each other if things go wrong – and help each other when things go well – in order to maximise the success. Put your personal pride into the melting pot and glory in the warm family feeling of a group that works closely together and shares a common goal.

Producer's role

A good luck card from the producer to the cast and to the backstage team will be welcomed, as will a brief personal appearance backstage to wish them all the best before the show. Resist any urge to nag. Everyone will be highly strung now; just tell them all that they have the makings of a great show and ask them to pull out all the stops and do their best.

Then retire to watch. It can be very unsettling standing out front and unable to contribute, feeling nervous for everyone and everything. While actors and back-stage team worry about their own individual appearances and responsibilities, the producer frets about every aspect of the production and is aware of each minute detail, good and bad. The other side of this coin is that, just like the anxieties, the exhilaration in a good production is also multiplied, a myriad cluster of nerves and pleasure, relief and sheer joy – and the excitement when a great show takes off is positively orgasmic.

All rehearsals can have their agonising moments but performing in front of an audience at last should make all the hard work worthwhile.

Problems and improvements

In an imperfect world, there are bound to be a few hiccups. The producer should not inflict any sweeping changes on the team now unless the situation is *really* desperate. But before the next performance he or she might, very tactfully, suggest a few minor improvements, bearing in mind that everyone's egos cry out to be pampered right now, not crushed, and that self confidence and tempers are particularly fragile at this stage.

Do not spoil the opening night by deprecating remarks. Most offenders will be only too well aware if they have let the side down in any way and will be apologising profusely for a late entrance or a missed cue, or a prop left in the wrong place. Be supportive and sympathetic, not acidly critical. Point out any problem areas that must be addressed but do so with humour and constructive help.

Pace

Audience response is wonderful, but it is a new ingredient and can be handled well or badly, especially laughter. The timing is all-important. Try to adapt your timing to the laughter, coming in with your next line as the crescendo is topped and just begins to crest – like a wave breaking. If you gabble on regardless, the laughter may drown vital lines. Moreover, the audience will not be able to relax and laugh properly if you cut them off *too* soon.

Generally, as the play rolls, first-night nerves are left behind, the routine becomes more familiar and the play should speed up. However, especially on the second night, there is often a feeling of anticlimax and the pace may slacken. Actors often blame the audience.

Audiences vary: some will be better than others and laugh more readily. Saturday-night audiences, and those with group bookings who create their own party atmosphere, are usually good. But often it is the cast who are to blame when an audience is less responsive than they hope. After the first-night high the players are tired and the launch excitement is over. If the next audience fail to laugh at that first great joke, the cast begin almost to resent them and, discouraged, do not give of their very best.

If an audience seems difficult, it is up to the players to take up the challenge and really sock it to them – not to drift into a half-hearted performance. This is where the producer may need to march backstage and jolly everyone into a more positive, attacking approach.

The dreaded speeches

At the end of the performance, do not inflict long speeches on an audience. These will detract horribly from the final flourish. If tradition dictates that you *have* to give the producer flowers or champagne publicly, make it *very, very* brief. If possible, tuck this in before the final resounding encore so that the show still finishes on a high.

Aftermath

Last-night party

Do see the show off in style. A party after the play with food and wine, friends and family, seals the success somehow. Party pieces – especially songs and odes about the production – can form the highlight of a post-play party and are bound to provoke lots of laughter. It adds to the zest of the occasion when everyone is busy scribbling away silly words in the dressing room and cajoling fellow actors to perform in their piece of entertainment.

This is a good opportunity for the backstage team and young offspring to have a go on stage too, and hidden talents of all kinds may be revealed.

Post-play depression

The last night is over. The exhilaration, the camaraderie and the frantic preparation have culminated in a run of good performances, and the glow of success is now fading. It is time to clear away the debris and think about next time.

Every play creates its own family of cast and backstage members whose talents, energies and enthusiasms link up for the duration of the production. Already the stories and anecdotes about this particular pantomime are fomenting in the pool of memories that form the folklore of the society, to be drawn upon in later years, to regale new members with 'Of course this was before your time, but there was once this hilarious situation when. . . '

There is always a sadness about parting company from good friends. As the players gather to sweep up, to tidy, to collect their personal belongings, each one is aware that now is the last time this particular set of people will be closely involved in this particular play. There will be changes next time and as the set is taken down, there is a funereal feel about the end of it all. It can seem almost sacrilegious to discuss the next set or the next costumes when this play is still not quite buried.

Compliments are shared and exchanged as the memories of this production still run fresh and are dipped into fondly. Sometimes there are even tears. The exchange of telephone numbers and signatures on programmes marks an attempt to keep the unit intact.

Planning ahead

When the hall is finally tidy and participants' cars bulge at the seams with boxes and bags of costumes, abandoned scripts, props, hired equipment and sundry lost property to return to their rightful owners, an adjournment to the pub is called for. Here the members can discuss the high points of this year's show and sow the seeds of enthusiasm for another show next year.

Some time soon it will be appropriate to discuss both the good and the bad points of the production, to analyse these so that the group can learn from its mistakes and build on the foundation of its strengths. Make lists of these strengths and weaknesses and draw up plans for the future, for instance:

Good points

Julie was discovered to have a good voice – need to capitalise on that next time.

A great finale – balloons worked really well.

Set changes went very smoothly – largely thanks to Howard's stage management and David's new rotating flats.

Bad points

Rita had trouble learning her lines – needs a smaller part or more help earlier.

There were jams front of house – more helpers needed, especially on Saturdays.

Publicity was weak – must start earlier next time.

Keep everyone involved

If the pantomime is one of several productions that the society perform each year, then doubtless a new play will be in rehearsal soon and energies will be channelled in that direction, keeping much of the membership busy again. However, pantomimes often involve far more people than do conventional plays so do not overlook the needs of those excess members who might like some continued involvement. (There will, of course, be those who wish to be left in peace for nine months or so.)

Perhaps your society is interested purely in an annual pantomime production. If so, it may help to maintain the group's entity by meeting occasionally between productions – perhaps for theatre visits (to professional shows and to other local amateur productions), workshops, social gatherings, or work parties to improve some aspect of the venue or build new flats or steps. There might also be fund-raising events, such as race nights or bingo – ostensibly to pay for new equipment but thoroughly enjoyable in their own right.

It is good to keep open by some means the lines of communication and continue the friendships and commitment established through the pantomime production.

The video party

Many groups reconvene for a viewing of the video of the production. (If the script is not your own, you may need to clear copyright. Check the smallprint.) A party will provide the excuse for a welcome reunion (perhaps about three weeks later, when members have had time to recover their energies). Allow time for the video to be processed and for any still photographs of the production to be numbered and labelled and put on boards or in an album, ready for taking orders. The party can be given a theme. It can be amusing to make it a sort of Oscar ceremony so that everyone dresses in style and silly awards are presented. For example:

Best scriptwriter
Nominations were received for:
Colin – for the ad-libbed rubbish he made up every evening;
Julie – for that wonderful speech off the top of her head when the panto horse failed to appear;
Peter – for rewriting *all* of his lines;

but the winner is *Henry* – for almost writing off the whole show when he fell off the end of the stage!

Best double act
Nominations were received for:
Grab and Bag the robbers – especially for the sausage scene;
The Ugly Sisters – who really made a complete balls-up of their parts;
Cinderella's silver shoes – who formed such a perfect duo to sweep her off her feet;

but the winners, for the most exciting double act in the show, are *Jean's boobs* – for daring to appear in that low-cut ball gown, when their performance fairly bounced along! They really rose to the occasion.

Keep up the momentum

Pantomimes are enormous fun. Try to keep that aspect and that energy alive in the society throughout the year.

13

Practical matters

The producer's role

No one knows everything about anything. Many directors and producers try to give the impression that they do but, ultimately, they have to entrust their cherished production to the experts who are devising and handling the technical aspects.

As the producer, you should know what you want, have a clear idea in your mind and then set out with the help of your backstage team to see how this effect might be achieved. Several very useful books are recommended in the Bibliography. The best backstage technicians will be supportive and rise to a challenge.

Make sure all the team use their imagination. There are many different ways to make a stage play exciting. Explore new ways to do things, to achieve better results and open up all sorts of fresh possibilities – this will be stimulating to all concerned. In order to be able to do so, however, it is important to start planning early and to involve the technical and other backstage experts right from the beginning. And then allow ample opportunity to experiment and try out any new ideas *in situ*.

How to organise the non-acting members of your group

Admit to your ignorance   Do not be afraid to lose face: if you do not understand something, say so – never pretend to understand and nod knowledgeably when you are in fact completely baffled by the jargon or technicalities.

Know what you want   Read through the script yet again. This time analyse carefully what you expect of the various departments and how you visualise each scene. Make notes during rehearsals as further ideas arise regarding:

staging and scenery
wardrobe
properties
lighting
sound
special effects
make-up.

Ask yourself these questions.

1. What sort of set do you want?
2. Is there a particular style that will give a coherent feel to the pantomime or to individual scenes? (For example, medieval, Victorian, flamboyant, understated, brightly coloured or in pastel shades, elegant, outrageous, silly, fun, sombre, crazy, soft and appealing, dream-like, nursery rhyme, 1920s, Dickensian.)
3. How can the various departments help you achieve this?

4. What is the particular atmosphere you are trying to create in each scene, as opposed to the overall play?
5. In general terms, how do you think you want the lighting to be in each scene?
6. More specifically, are there any special moments that might be helped by a lighting effect?
7. What sort of costumes do you think will work best – both for general effects and for each particular character in each particular scene? Are changes necessary?
8. Are there any particular colour schemes or effects which will help and which might need contributions from costume, lighting and set painting?
9. How can sound help – and when?
10. How do you see each prop in your mind? (It is no good yelling at the last minute when the teacup you visualised was five feet high, made of polystyrene, and the props people have produced a pretty little porcelain teacup from Grandma's dresser.)
11. What kind of make-up is needed for each character?

If you have duly considered these details and thought through all the possible decisions and consequences, then you will be in a strong position to discuss your ideas with the parties concerned.

Communicate   Having analysed your vision of each scene, communicate your ideas to each department clearly. Listen and share ideas. While always holding on to the integrity of your overall vision of the play or scenes, do discuss and be prepared to consider the experts' suggestions and think again. They probably have much to contribute so do not squash any idea without giving it due consideration. With luck, you will all inspire each other – enthusiasm is highly contagious!

Staging and Scenery

No two plays are alike, and there is a vast amount of difference between a drawing-room drama box set and the scenery for a pantomime. First decide on the overall style of the play. Then, for each scene, the set designer should consider:

What is the particular effect required?
What colour(s) will be most effective?
How can the scenery be made interesting?
How fast is each scene change?
Should it be realistic or fantastic?
What will it cost?
How much room is there?
What material and construction methods are most suitable?
What fundamentals must be incorporated for the purposes of the plot?
Are there any vital props to be born in mind or incorporated into the design?

Plan of campaign

1. Read play.
2. Discuss ideas with producer.
3. Research useful information and illustrative material.
4. Sketch out rough ideas.
5. Build model of set and refine detailed scale drawings of scenes.
6. Discuss with producer and rest of team.
7. Order any materials necessary.

8. Construct set.
9. Paint set.
10. Ensure stage manager and team are aware of set-change details.
11. Technical rehearsals.
12. Strike and store scenery.

Making a storybook with turning pages part of the scenery is one way to effect quick scene changes.

Basic set requirements

Here is some basic gen for the producer who is inexperienced in backstage technicalities and does not want to feel like a complete idiot when the jargon starts to flow. For those who are already well informed, perhaps this brief summary may prove a useful reminder of all the possibilities and a trigger to new ideas.

Flats   These can be made of timber framework with canvas, cotton duck, hessian, heavy-duty cardboard, gauze or muslin, polystyrene, MDF board – various thicknesses available. Composition board, blockboard foam board and hardboard can also be used in various ways. But bear in mind that hardboard is very heavy.

Not a conventional idea but one can work very well is to hang relatively slim flats so that they can be turned. This obviates the need for individual timber framing and allows the flats to be swivelled for quick scene changes. The flats can also be put on to runners.

Apart from the basic flats, filler flats may be needed for special purposes, such as windows, doors, arches and fireplaces.

All the materials must be fireproofed before use.

Wings are those bits that stick out at the side, which actors cower behind immediately before their entrances. They are excellent for large stages but are not essential and do

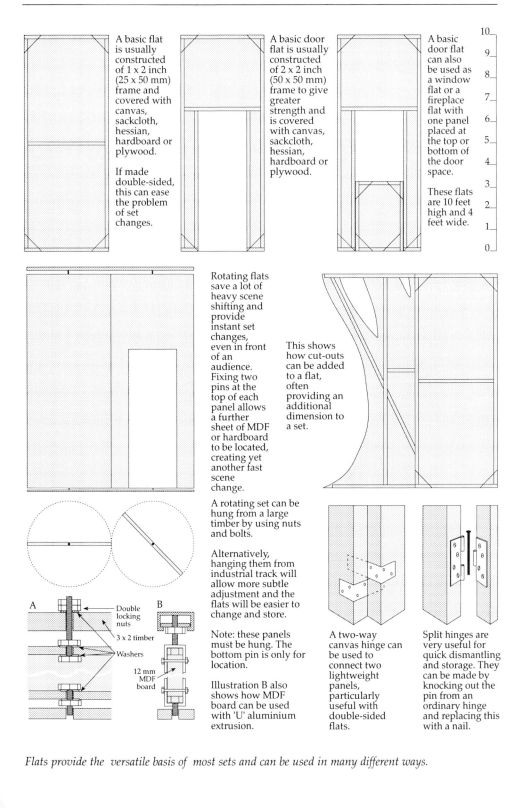

A basic flat is usually constructed of 1 x 2 inch (25 x 50 mm) frame and covered with canvas, sackcloth, hessian, hardboard or plywood.

If made double-sided, this can ease the problem of set changes.

A basic door flat is usually constructed of 2 x 2 inch (50 x 50 mm) frame to give greater strength and is covered with canvas, sackcloth, hessian, hardboard or plywood.

A basic door flat can also be used as a window flat or a fireplace flat with one panel placed at the top or bottom of the door space.

These flats are 10 feet high and 4 feet wide.

Rotating flats save a lot of heavy scene shifting and provide instant set changes, even in front of an audience. Fixing two pins at the top of each panel allows a further sheet of MDF or hardboard to be located, creating yet another fast scene change.

This shows how cut-outs can be added to a flat, often providing an additional dimension to a set.

A rotating set can be hung from a large timber by using nuts and bolts.

Alternatively, hanging them from industrial track will allow more subtle adjustment and the flats will be easier to change and store.

A   Double locking nuts   B
3 x 2 timber
Washers
12 mm MDF board

Note: these panels must be hung. The bottom pin is only for location.

Illustration B also shows how MDF board can be used with 'U' aluminium extrusion.

A two-way canvas hinge can be used to connect two lightweight panels, particularly useful with double-sided flats.

Split hinges are very useful for quick dismantling and storage. They can be made by knocking out the pin from an ordinary hinge and replacing this with a nail.

Flats provide the versatile basis of most sets and can be used in many different ways.

occupy a lot of precious space on a small stage. Drapes or flats that box the set, with gaps for entrances, leave a larger acting area. The sight lines must be borne in mind and screened, however marginally. In any event, always make sure your actors are well trained so that they do not hover in view of the audience.

Ground rows and cut-outs are two-dimensional pieces of scenery, independent of the flats, which can be used to establish quick scene changes and/or to hide incompatible pieces of equipment or staging, such as a ramp, steps or a special piece of lighting.

Different levels of height stimulate interest and help the producer to group actors in a more pleasing variety of ways. Consider the use of raised areas (rostra) and split levels, blocks, platforms, trucks (mobile platforms set on castors) and steps of various shapes and sizes – both on the stage and leading up to it.

Drapes and hangings can be used for numerous effects.

Curtains can be used in combination with flats.

A cyclorama or **skycloth** might be a smooth plastered wall or a stretched backcloth (curved or straight) which can be lit interestingly.

Backcloths and **drops** can be hung and may be 'flown' if there is sufficient ceiling space above the stage and a sound, safe structure capable of supporting the weight.

Gauzes which let light through will allow for transformation scenes and ghostly effects.

Glitter curtains give a superb sparkling effect. Different colours are available and the silver ones can be lit in exciting ways. Their reflective quality and shimmering movement opens up all sorts of possibilities. Hung right across the sides of the stage, they can also be used instead of wings.

Quick changes can be achieved in various ways. Try some of the following:

Transformation scenes with gauze.

Flats that are hung and can swivel.

Flats on runners (like sliding doors).

Hinged flats (rather like an old-fashioned screen) with scenes on both sides.

Layers of lightweight flats that can be quickly located on to pins on the main base flats.

A trucked four-sided unit, with each face presenting a different scene.

Canvas or material. This might be on a roller that can be dropped or it might be flown. (Heavyweight cartridge paper of the kind used for photographic backgrounds can also be used. It is available in 9-feet or 12-feet widths.)

Independent cut-outs can also suggest a scene in the simplest way possible and are especially useful in brief front-of-curtain scenes – for example, Dick Whittington's milestone or Cinderella's coach.

Design and painting

Perspective is of great importance. The designer must first establish the eye level of the viewer. Is the audience sitting below or on raised seating? Where do you want their eyes to focus? Parallel or converging lines will create the effect of perspective. But be careful! If the perspective is overdone, the actors who stand at the back will look like giants.

Scale drawings of the set designs provide the best starting point for the set design blueprints. Measure the size of the stage area to be painted. Decide whether the scale is to be metric or imperial. Draw out the area on paper one tenth of the actual size (for metric) or with one inch representing every foot (for imperial), and

Using perspective in the sets can help to suggest space and distance, even on a tiny stage.

complete the drawing within this area. Photocopy or trace this drawing so as not to damage the original. The copy can then be squared up with a grid (like graph paper), with each square either one tenth actual size or one inch square.

Transferring the designs Give the flats a white coat of paint first. This helps the colours to be true and to have more luminosity. When the paint is dry, place the flats on the floor. The designer should then grab some willing soul to help manipulate the chalk line. This is a taut string generously coated with chalk; proprietary ones can be bought. By stretching the cord across the flats at one foot intervals and then plucking it, straight lines of chalk are transferred on to the flats to divide them up into one-foot squares (or a convenient metric unit, say 25cm).

Mark both the scale drawings and the flats like a map grid, with numbers along the top and letters down the sides so that those doing the drawing can locate which square they are working within. It is then relatively easy even for uninitiated set painters to reproduce a rough outline of the drawing, square by square, in pencil. Provide several copies of the squared-up design so that several people can work at once.

The designer can alter or improve this guideline before setting about the painting proper. If time is short, helpers can fill in an outline with paint under the guidance of the set designer – like painting by numbers.

Painting Watercolours or matte household emulsion paint are probably the simplest to use. Special colours can be mixed in do-it-yourself supermarkets or paint suppliers. Masking with tape, which can be peeled off when the paint is dry, is a useful way to create stripes or divide up areas of different colour.

Be bold. This is pantomime! Do not be afraid of colour or daunted by the size and scale involved.

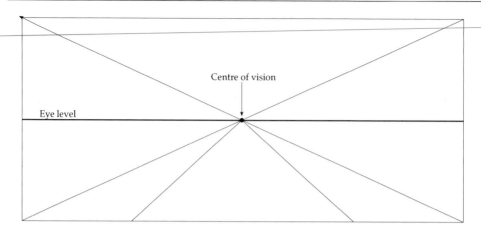

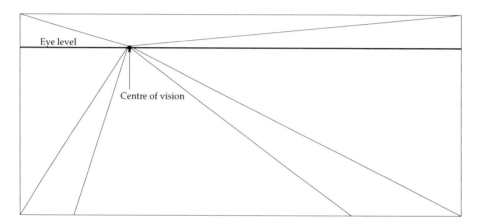

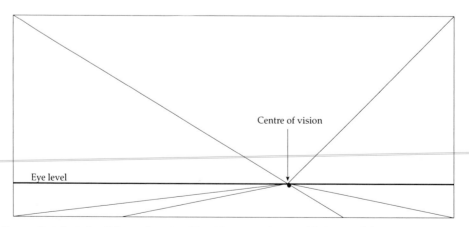

Even quite talented artists can have trouble with perspective yet this is one of the most important factors in adding dimension to a stage setting. First decide on the eye level and then on the centre of vision – and do not forget to include the ground or floor as these help enormously to increase the feeling of size and distance.

Do not waste time unnecessarily. Remember, in most scenes, the attention is mainly on the actors. Do not spend copious amounts of time on infinite detail which cannot be seen by most of the audience. This is especially wasteful if the scene is one that is always full of people. In a crowd scene, concentrate on the areas above the actors' heads.

Costume

The main factors to consider are:
>What is the overall style, period, and ethnic background of the play?
>What features must be incorporated for the purposes of the plot?
>What colour(s) or colour scheme(s) will be most effective?
>Is there a strong set colour to bear in mind?
>How will costumes help to establish character?
>Are there any fast costume changes?
>Is there anything already in stock that is suitable or can be adapted?
>What will it cost?

Plan of campaign

1. Read play.
2. Discuss ideas with producer.
3. Research useful information and illustrative material.
4. Sketch out rough ideas.
5. Check through existing wardrobe.
6. Discuss ideas with producer and rest of team.
7. Buy any materials necessary.
8. Recruit and instruct any helpers.
9. Measure cast.
10. Make costumes or arrange to hire them well ahead of first rehearsal.
11. Try costumes on cast.
12. Alter as necessary.
13. Work out logistics of quick changes.
14. Supervise costumes at dress rehearsals. Check everything looks OK out front.
15. Be on hand during performances to help with any fast changes. Take a needle, cotton, scissors and safety pins for any last-minute repairs.
16. After show, gather in everything safely and then clean, repair and return items as necessary.

Making the costumes

If dresses are made up as separate tops and bottoms, they can be more readily adjusted to suit different-shaped performers on future occasions. Make separate collars and cuffs to dress up basic tops. A variety of layers with overskirts, aprons, frills and ruffles can dress up skirts to suit different situations. Elasticised waistbands mean the costumes will fit a greater variety of waistlines and are also good for fast changes. Or use curtain tape on waists, sleeves and necklines so that these can be gathered in as tightly or as loosely as required. Velcro fastenings will help fast changes, too. Avoid zips, which can jam in a moment of panic.

Do not waste unnecessary time. Make the clothes basically very simple. To convey a particular period or style, concentrate on the shape and silhouette of the costume. Do not fuss over details and finishing. The overall impression is all that counts. Use fairly large stitches that can be undone easily if a costume must be altered. If time is really running out, seams and hems can be glued.

Make animal costumes from basic fur or skin-type bodies with interchangeable heads or masks so that they are more versatile. If the actor has to talk or sing, make sure the costume allows for this and, in any event, ensure the actor can see clearly and be heard.

Medieval and nursery-rhyme costumes of various kinds, including peasants, kings, queens and barons, suit many of the pantomime themes. Add those with an Eastern flavour, like Sinbad and Aladdin, and a few dressier Restoration Cinderella styles, and you will have the basis of a good pantomime wardrobe. Other stand-by characters are sundry gypsies and pirates (do collect headscarves), fairies and villains with swirling cloaks, cannibals and witches.

Scour jumble sales for:

jewellery (the flashier the better)

gloves, scarves, hats, bags, shoes and other accessories

cloaks and capes

tights

baggy trousers (they can be converted into breeches)

brightly coloured skirts and dresses

men's shirts (biggish white ones can be left white or dyed, and/or turned into jolly good pirate or musketeer shirts by adding full sleeves)

evening gowns (sources of rich-looking material)

sequins, buttons, feathers, lace, buckles, ribbons, braid and trimming of any kind

curtains and bedspreads, furniture fabric and hessian, old sheets and blankets (good material in bulk)

net curtaining for fairy tutus and wings, harem pantaloons and the like

old fur coats for animal costumes

Properties

The main factors to consider are:

What is the style and period of the play?

Is the property list comprehensive?

Does it present any particular difficulties?

Which, if any, pieces might be seen as part of the set design?

Are there any fast scene changes that must be worked out well in advance?

Which props are essential to the plot and which ones are there just for fun?

Is there anything already in stock that is suitable or can be adapted?

What will the different items cost to procure or make?

Whom can you nab to help you make the props?

Will anything have to be hired?

Plan of campaign

1. Read play.
2. Discuss ideas with producer and set designer.
3. Research useful information and illustrative material.
4. Draw up lists and sketch out rough ideas for anything that has to be made specially.
5. Check through existing properties.
6. Discuss ideas with producer and rest of team.
7. Ask cast and team if they can provide any of the necessary items or materials.
8. Buy any materials necessary.
9. Recruit and instruct any helpers.
10. Make new items.
11. Make sure these are approved by producer and/or set designer.
12. Supervise props at dress and technical rehearsals. Check everything looks OK out front.
13. Organise properties throughout performances.
14. After show, gather in everything safely and then clean, repair and return items as necessary.

Develop the habit of collecting anything that might be useful. Consider the use of the following materials:

paper, tissue and papier-mâché	plaster of Paris
cardboard	egg cartons
hardboard	felt and fabrics
MDF board	corrugated plastic
foam board	upholstery
cotton wool	webbing ropes and cord
polystyrene	plywood
flour and water (baked dough)	timber of all kinds
Fimo for small items	doweling
fibreglass	old containers, tins, bottles and jars
paper bags	coconut halves
wire and netting	any scrap material you come across
metal foil,	
zinc and aluminium	

Hints and tips

To help fast scene changes, keep everything fairly lightweight but stable. If props are static and not moved during the show (say, a row of bottles and jars on a shelf), they can be glued on.

Make plans of the stage and map out prop positions carefully, marking the stage floor for fast, accurate positioning. Properties add to the fun of the production. Make them colourful, oversized and as humorous as possible. Absurdity will not go amiss in a pantomime.

Be imaginative and resourceful and you will not need to spend too much money.

Do not waste time. Keep outlines and any decoration or painting simple and uncluttered. Lettering should be big and bold so that it can be read by most of the audience, not just those in the front row.

Various stages in the creation of the Giant's boots

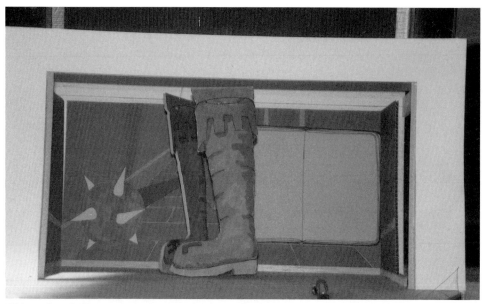

The small-scale boots are tested out on the model of the stage.

The full-size boots are cut out from a sheet of polystyrene.

Standard props for pantomime

'Boo', 'Hiss' and 'Aaah' boards
cauldrons
clouds and rocks

crowns and swords
food and drink; sausages
jugs and tankards

The finished boots are flown above the stage, along with the Giant's pizza.

The boots perform.

scrolls (for herald's announcements)
signposts and milestones
trees and flowers

tree stumps
wands (for fairy,
wizard and witch)

Lighting

The main factors to consider are:

What is the overall style of and approach to the pantomime?
(For instance, is it to be traditional or futuristic?)
Is there any theme to the production which can be helped by the lighting; for example, by colour schemes or the lighting of specific areas?
How much power supply is available?
Is the existing lighting rig able to meet the immediate requirements of the production?
Does any new equipment need to be bought or hired?

Then, for each scene, the lighting designer should ask:

What is the particular effect (or effects) required?
What time of day is it?
What is the mood in this scene (for example, happy or gloomy)?
Will a colour filter help give the right effect?
Where are the actors standing?
Which other parts of the stage need to be lit?
Will any specially set lanterns or spots be required?
Should the lighting be realistic or magical?

Plan of campaign

1. Read play.
2. Discuss ideas with producer and set designer.
3. Research information and ideas on how to achieve effects.
4. Make lighting plot.
5. Check existing equipment.
6. Discuss ideas with producer and rest of team.
7. Attend rehearsals to check out appropriateness of ideas and incorporate any changes into lighting plot.
8. Borrow, buy, make or organise the hire of any equipment needed.
9. If applicable, discuss requirements and areas of responsibility with electricians and any lighting assistants. Make a timetable.
10. Set up the electric wiring, appliances and lighting as needed.
11. Check safety and focusing of lanterns.
12. Supervise lighting at dress and technical rehearsals. Check that everything works well and looks as you hoped, and that the producer, set designer, wardrobe and stage manager are all happy with the results too.
13. Make any adjustments.
14. Oversee lighting throughout performances.
15. After show, if necessary, take the lighting rig down safely and return or store equipment as required.

Basic lighting angles and equipment

Front light is direct on to the face and flattens the features. It can be used to eliminate shadows cast by the eye socket but generally it is best to aim at a 45-degree angle, which is far more flattering.

Key light provides the main source of light in any scene.

Fill light fills in any areas of shadow.

Side light helps to light the actors' faces when they face the wings and to give solidity and roundness to the face. It may also be used to suggest beams of sun or moonlight streaming on to the stage.

Cross light is very shallow or horizontal side light.

Back light does not affect an actor's face and so it is useful for filling background areas with colour. It may create a halo effect around an actor.

Top or down light can be used for dramatic effects as it picks out certain protruding features, such as a wide brimmed hat or a sword.

Bottom or up lights (or footlights) used to be called floats, from the days when oil wicks were floated on water or oil to avoid the risk of fire. Originally devised to show off dancers' legs, uplights give an eerie, shadowy effect and can be very dramatic for, say, lighting a villain or demon. They can also be used to create low-level sky effects such as a sunset or horizon.

Profile spot This very efficient lantern gives a hard-edged, intense beam of light. Manipulation of the beam by gates and shutters allows it to be narrowed and concentrated or less intense and with softer edges.

Fresnel spot This creates a soft-edged beam with less harsh edges; the beam can be shaped by barn doors.

Pebble convex lantern Similar to a Fresnel but with a convex lens which diffuses the light and makes the beam semi hard-edged and without flare.

Par Gives an intense parallel beam like a car headlight. It is good as a key light and for strong effects like sunlight.

Flood Covers large areas and so is excellent for lighting backcloths, on battens to form a strip or in ground rows as footlights.

Gel colour filter These were once made of gelatine but are now of plastic. Traditionally the fairy in pantomime is lit in a pretty pink light and the demon in ghastly green or fiery red.

Gobo patterns or designs A gobo is a metal plate with a pattern or shape cut out or etched from it. You can make your own from thin metal cut just a few inches taller than the gate. (Printer's litho plate is excellent but aluminium foil take-away plates will do.) When a suitably pierced gobo is fitted in front of a profile spot, textures and images are projected on to the stage and can suggest dappled woodland light, a medieval skyline, windows, clouds, leaves, a distant palace or castle and so on.

Using a series of slightly different gobos on different lanterns and flashing each one in turn so that they chase each other can create moving images and might suggest a cascading fountain or wildly waving tree branches in a storm.

Moving images can be created via special painted glass discs set in front of a projector. These can be hired and create wonderful clouds, snow, water, rain, smoke and fire.

Stars can be imitated by a gobo or a star slide in a projector. Alternatively, tiny pea bulbs or clear Christmas-tree bulbs can be wired up and then pierced though a 'star cloth. Or a veritable galaxy of hanging stars can be made from a myriad balls of foil suspended on black thread and then lit by side, top or back lighting to twinkle very effectively.

Ultraviolet light combined with fluorescent paint can give magical effects. Be careful that there is no light spill from anywhere else and use only a stage UV light (*never* a medical lamp, which may damage skin or eyes). There are all sorts of exciting possibilities. White skeletons or ghosts can glow and dance in the dark, animals' eyes appear gleaming through forest trees, fairies appear and costumes glow mysteriously.

Coloured torches Provided a complete blackout can be achieved, a well-rehearsed group of actors or dancers dressed in black can achieve magic effects with coloured torches that whirl and mingle and flash from the blackness.

Strobe lighting This can be used only for a short period of time as it affects the sense of balance and may induce epileptic fits in those so prone. However, used sensibly, the flashing strobe light can give a very dramatic result, seeming to make actors move in a rapid and jerky manner, like a silent movie.

Silhouettes and dramatic shadows can be achieved by lighting just the background or by back-lighting a smoke screen, gauze or sheet of material.

Gauze transformations Stunning magical effects can be created by gradually reducing front light on a gauze and simultaneously bringing up back light on a scene or person behind. Solid walls simply melt away and a new scene or a character supposedly far away – or, perhaps, a ghost – appears.

Control board This is the 'nerve centre' of the lighting system, with all the various lanterns and groups of lights plugged into it, including the house lights in the auditorium. It generally contains dimmers which allow lights to be gradually brightened or dimmed so that different lighting effects can be faded in and out.

Sound

Sound effects can be created manually as required or prerecorded and played back at the appropriate moment.

On-the-spot sound effects

The old-fashioned methods may not be so sophisticated but are none the less very effective and appropriate to use in pantomime. They are reliable because they are less prone to technical hitches and less complicated if the actors skip a page or so.

It can also be great fun as the sound personnel hover in the wings with:

buckets of water to pour into metal containers below
tins of dried peas for rain
flexible metal thunder sheets (suitably amplified, a good thunder sheet takes a lot of
   beating – in more ways than one! Actually it is shaken, not beaten, and needs to be
   firmly fixed so that it can be prevented from thundering when not in use)
coconut shells for horses' hooves
cap guns and starting pistols (a gun licence may be needed)
boxes full of broken glass to shake
whistles, bells, gongs and football rattles
door knockers on hunks of wood

Audibility can be a problem, especially if the curtains are heavy or there is any other barrier that muffles sound. A loudspeaker may be useful to counteract this problem. Space can also be a limitation if the wing area is cramped.

Of course, you can always send the whole thing up and do the sounds effects in full view of the audience, or hold out notices saying 'SPLASH!' and 'BANG!'. Or even invite the audience up to help.

The musicians can help enormously too: a pianist and drummer can suggest all sorts of bangs, crashes, tinkling bells and so on; electronic keyboards offer any amount of background and foreground sounds, like waves washing on a desert island shore or harps playing.

Recorded sound effects

Using prerecorded sound effects offers a huge variety of exciting possibilities. Sound effects can be created specifically and recorded in readiness or bought in and mixed to suit. They are available on record, tape or compact disc in shops and libraries. If you need to manufacture your own sound effects, remember to leave a decent gap between the various effects on your tape. Tape more than you think you need so that the sound effect never runs out too soon (it is a simple matter to fade it out when no longer needed). And check the volume levels carefully in rehearsal so that you neither deafen your audience nor leave them straining to hear.

Plan of campaign

1. Read play and highlight when sound effects are needed.
2. Discuss requirements with producer and any other technical staff with whom you might need to coordinate (for example, thunder and lightning would involve the lighting team too). Check what music is needed for pre-performance and during intervals.
3. Research possibilities on how to achieve effects.
4. Make sound plot.
5. Attend rehearsals to check out appropriateness of ideas and incorporate any changes or additions into the sound plot.
6. Borrow, buy, make or hire any effects or equipment needed.
7. If using taped sound, mix sounds as needed and make up tape with sound effects in correct order. Mark sound plot clearly with the final positions of each sound on the tape.
8. Supervise sound effects at dress and technical rehearsals. Make any necessary adjustments. Finalise coordination with the stage manager and the rest of the backstage crew.
9. Be there early on the performance nights – in good time to check everything is in order and to have apt welcoming music playing in house as the first members of the audience arrive.

Special Effects

Pantomimes are based on fairy stories and fantasy. Magical effects are part of this and will add enormously to the fun of the show and the entrancement of the children. Often the effects do not occur sufficiently frequently to require the constant attention of somebody in the wings, and so the effects may be contrived by the stage manager, lighting, sound or props crew, a combination of them all or by a specific person who pops up as needed, under the stage manager's jurisdiction.

Like the sound and lighting, the special effects should be highlighted in the play copy. Discuss how these might best be achieved and whose responsibility they will ultimately become. Generally they will be included in the stage manager's prompt copy and allotted to one or various parties in the most suitable way, depending on whether the effect is being generated by lights, sound or even pyrotechnics.

Have fun with some of the following:

Dry ice This is frozen carbon dioxide, which produces a heavy vapour when melted in boiling water.

Smoke Smoke can also be produced by special guns and machines. Apart from suggesting steam trains, clouds, fog, swirling mist and a fire in the vicinity, smoke can be combined with lighting effects to 'seed the air' and add to the effectiveness of light 'curtains' and beams of light.

Flashes and bangs Maroons and flash powder are potentially very dangerous and a licence is required before explosives can be used or stored. In a small building with many people milling about, it is safer to use pre-recorded bangs. For the same reason, it is best to hire a proper flash box rather than making your own. Any kind of 'pyrotechnics' can be expensive and should be treated with caution and respect – but the impact on the audience is terrific! Alternatively – and less expensively – professional photographic flash guns can be combined with coloured lights and smoke for magical effects, such as when the genie appears from Aladdin's lamp or the fairy waves her wand.

Transformation powder This slow-burning powder produces a flame in a variety of colours – green or amber, for example. It should be kept in a metal container and lit by a taper.

Snow This can be suggested by various lighting effects or created by lots of paper dots released from a snow bag above the stage. This looks good as the flakes float gently down, but it is best used at the end of a scene or act so there is opportunity to sweep up the mess afterwards.

Transparencies These can help to set a scene and act as a backdrop on a darkened stage or be projected on to a more restricted area, either on the stage or at the side (which avoids some of the problems that arise when other lighting 'kills' the effect). Back projection may be considered to avoid interruption by objects or people in front.

Ripple machines (or projectors) incorporate a tube into which ripple patterns have been cut. This rotates in front of a light source and creates gentle rippling waves of light – lovely for underwater scenes!

Mirrors can create flashing lights on a stage, just as the many facets on a spinning globe in a disco have a fascinating effect. A hexagonal arrangement of mirrors revolving on a slow gramophone turntable and lit by a spot can flash across the stage and suggest, for example, the windows of a passing train.

Try to finish with a flourish. An exciting special effect can help give the show a final piece of magic. Simple party ideas can also be very effective. Ticker-tape streamers and party poppers introduce noise and celebration – and masses of balloons can flood the stage with colour. Throw 'snowballs' into the audience, wave banners and glitter sticks, and find different ways to generate energy and festivity.

Make-up

Most make-up artists revel in pantomime. It is an opportunity to experiment with dramatic and exciting make-up. In small theatres, generally, the make-up has to be fairly restrained for conventional plays, so panto offers a grand excuse to let rip for once.

Not only are there books devoted to this subject in depth, there are also courses offered to members of amateur societies by both regional experts and such renowned sources of information as the Royal Shakespeare Company.

The kit

You will need some of the following, and boxes with dividers to keep everything together.

A range of brushes, from fine eyeliner tips and lip brushes to plump rouge mops
make-up remover and tissues
cotton wool balls and cotton buds
powder puffs
foundations in various shades – these can be greasepaint, stick, cake or liquid bases
sticks or pots of lining colours for adding detail
rouge; face powder
eye shadow – powder, cream, liquid and pencil in a variety of colours; mascara
eyebrow pencils
eyeliners – pencil, cake and liquid; false eyelashes
liquid body make-up
crepe for false beards, moustaches, eyebrows and stubble; latex and Derma Wax for
   special effects such as scars and warts; false fingernails (useful for witches and
   Eastern potentates)
false noses of various shapes and sizes
nose putty
spirit gum
wigs and hairpieces
black tooth enamel
clown white
stage blood; scissors
hair bands, grips and pins
towels
water

The more specialised items will accumulate as they are needed. Many make-up boxes are launched with a basic stock of foundation, powder and cleansing cream, augmented by the cast's own make-up and leftovers from various sources. This initial stock will gradually be added to and replaced over the years.

Plan of campaign

1. Read play.
2. Analyse appearance of characters.
3. Discuss overall style and aims of production and the essence of individual characters with both the producer and the actors concerned.
4. Research any necessary background information and how to achieve effects.
5. Make plot of timing, noting any fast changes or when many people will need help with their make-up at once.
6. Attend rehearsals to check out appropriateness of ideas and incorporate any changes or additions.
7. Check through stock and buy any new make-up required.
8. Arrange hire of wigs.
9. Organise any extra help needed and plan who is doing what when.
10. Supervise make-up and hair styling at dress rehearsals. Allow ample opportunity to practise any specially difficult or previously untried types of make-up. Check effect out front and make any necessary adjustments. Finalise coordination with the rest of the make-up team.

11. Be there early on performance nights. Allow plenty of time to make up the cast for the opening scene and to concentrate on any particularly complicated characters. Be well organised for any quick changes.

12. After the final performance, tidy up and collect everything together, noting any items that need replacement and returning wigs to hire companies.

Hints and tips

Use shadows and highlights. Much of the effectiveness of make-up depends on light and shade, on its sculpturing qualities, rather than just its colour. For example, lines alone will not age a face convincingly. Create the effect of sagging jaws, eye-bags, creases, folds and wrinkles with shadows and highlights, first asking the actors to grin widely and to furrow their brows so that their own natural lines can be detected.

To black out teeth, use proper black tooth enamel. Anything else will not adhere properly to the surface of a tooth and will wash or rub off.

Ensure the make-up stays where it belongs. Drawing a moustache on a face can look awful and is potentially disastrous if the actor has to play a love scene: he is likely to leave the heroine with a blackened face. Similarly, too much foundation or lipstick can be deposited on costumes and other faces, so if the actors have an imminent close encounter, it is especially important to make sure any excess is removed beforehand. And do ensure that wigs, beards, moustaches and false noses are stuck on very firmly, too. Do not skimp and leave the performers at risk of, literally, losing face in front of the audience.

Use optical illusions to your advantage. Horizontal shadows and lines will widen and flatten a face, while vertical ones will narrow and lengthen. In the same way that lots of little divisions make a line look longer, accentuating eyelashes with mascara makes eyes look bigger. Light areas always look bigger and dark areas smaller.

A little sparkle or glitter will add glamour to a fairy's make-up. A red sequin on the centre of each eyelid will give the demon king an occasional extra fiery flash of light. Do not forget to make up the neck and hands.

Final thoughts

There is much more to examine and discover. This section merely contains a few ideas and starting points to fire the imagination. Ingenuity and inventiveness are far more important than expensive equipment. Some of the suggestions included here should encourage novice producers and backstage personnel to appreciate just how much can be contributed by a keen and imaginative backstage team. Think laterally, be positive, research, read books and drama magazines, ask questions, seek the advice of other societies, and experiment until ways are found to achieve the desired effects. Help each other as much as possible. It is this pooling of expertise and enthusiasm to a common end – a successful production – that will turn the commonplace play into something really stunning.

Good luck! Or perhaps I should say, 'Break a leg!'

Bibliography and further reading

Avril Lethbridge, *Act Now* Frederick Warne 1979

Martyn Hepworth, *Amateur Drama: production and management*
B T Batsford 1978

Michael Green, *The Art of Coarse Acting* Hutchinson (& Arrow Books Ltd) 1964

Susan Date and Kelvin Watson, *Come Down Stage* Pelham Books 1971

Rosemary Ingham and Liz Covey, *The Costume Designer's Handbook*
Prentice Hall Inc. USA 1983

Sheila Jackson, *Costumes for the Stage* The Herbert Press 1978

Jacquie Govier, *Create your own Stage Costume* A & C Black 1995

Douglas Young, *Create your own Stage Faces* Bell and Hyman 1985

Tim Streader and John A Williams, *Create your own Stage Lighting*
Bell and Hyman 1985

Jacquie Govier, *Create your own Stage Props* A & C Black 1984

Terry Thomas, *Create your own Stage Sets* A & C Black 1985

Graham Walne, *Effects for the Theatre A & C Black* 1995

David Pickering, *Encyclopaedia of Pantomime* Gale Research International 1993

Ole Bruun-Rasmussen and Gret Petersen, *Make-up, Costumes and Masks for the Stage*
Sterling Publishing Co. Inc. USA 1976

Katherine Strand Holkboer, *Patterns for Theatrical Costume* Prentice Hall Inc. 1984

Ivan Butler, *Producing Pantomime and Revue* W & G Foyle Limited 1962

Chris Hoggett, *Stage Crafts* A & C Black 1975

Richard Corson, *Stage Makeup* Prentice Hall Inc. 1981

Rosemary Swinfield, *Stage Make-up step-by-step* A & C Black 1995

Index

A Christmas Carol 115
absentees 17, 20, 53, 54, 55, 84-5
accents 73
acts 26, 27, 69, 100,
ad lib 19, 75, 76,
advance bookings and information 95, 96
advertising 101 *see also* publicity
aftermath 119-21
Aladdin 6, 31, 74, 86, 108-11, 113, 114, 130, 138
Alderman Fitzwarren 112, 113
Ali Baba and the Forty Thieves 113, 114
Alice Fitzwarren 113
Alice in Wonderland 108, 112, 115
Alice through the Looking Glass 115
Ancient Rome 6, 7
animals 10, 73, 104, 111-12, 113, 130
archiving 99
areas of the stage 56
audibility 49, 74, 136
audience 7, 12, 18, 19, 50-1, 67, 69, 70, 74, 76, 77, 80, 86-93, 94-5, 103, 105, 111, 117, 137 *see also* audience participation
audience participation, 19, 77, 86-93, 103, 108, 110, 116
audience, relaxing the 77, 87
audition form 15, 21
audition pieces 17
auditions 15-22

Babes in the Wood 86, 110, 113, 114
backcloth 126
backstage 15
  team 25, 27 34-50, 53, 62, 68, 69, 76, 116, 117, 119, 122-40
Baddies 6 , 8, 92, 110, 111, 113, 130, 135
ballet 6
banners 102
Baron Hardup 112, 113
Beauty and the Beast 110
beginners *see* newcomers
beginning 12, 87,
blocking moves 55-8,
body movement 71, 72, 78
booby traps 17
booking forms 95
booking the hall 23,
budget 8, 30-2, 93
buttons 90, 111, 113

calendar 25
Captain Hook 112
cast 8, 15, 20-1, 25, 27, 48, 53, 62-4. 69, 80, 82, 116, 119, 13ı
cast list 9, 101
casting 15-21, 88
catering 51 *see also* food and drink
cats 112, 113
character 11, 12, 14, 16, 26-7, 48, 59, 67, 70-1, 73, 90, 105, 111, 129, 139
children 7, 10, 64, 70, 77, 91, 100, 103, 105, 108, 111, 119
choreography 64, 81-2
chorus 20, 21, 26, 67, 79-80, 82-5
Cinderella 6, 13, 77, 86, 89, 91, 108, 110-14, 126, 130
classic pantomime exchanges 77, 90
clown 6, 110
Columbine 6
comics and comedy *see* humour
communication 25, 29, 121
comperes 88
contrasts 19, 78, 104
Cook 108, 113
copyright 24, 80, 121
costume 39-40, 64-6, 94, 104, 122, 123, 129-30
costume changes 9, 39, 66, 129
courses 78, 138
Cow 111-12, 113
criticism 63, 68-9, 118
crowd scenes 82-5, 64
cues 35, 47, 59, 62, 64, 67, 68, 118
curtains 37, 38, 123, 126
cut outs 126
cyclorama 126

Dame Trot 108, 113
Dame Twankey 6, 113
dames 65, 73, 78, 81, 90, 91, 108-9, 113
dance 20, 79, 81-2, 104, 111
Dandino 6 *see also* Prince Charming
delivery 75
demon 6, 113, 135
Demon King 110, 113, 140
Dick Whittington 86, 108-10, 112-14, 126
diction 74
director 15 *see also* producer
discipline 62, 63, 84, 106
double acts 78, 111, 121
dress rehearsals 25, 65-9, 88, 129, 131, 137, 139
dressing room 89, 105, 106, 117
duos *see* double acts

electrics 24, 35, 134
emergencies 38, 40, 88-9, 129
Emperor's Nightingale, The 112, 114

emperors 31, 112
encores 67
entrances 57, 58, 62, 67, 68, 72, 118, 125
exercise 71, 74
exits 14, 57, 68, 72, 74
expressions 72, 85, 111

fairies 73, 91, 110, 113, 130, 137, 138, 140
fairy tales 7
final rehearsal 68-9
finale 12, 66, 106, 120
fire regulations 23, 43
first impressions 86
first night *see* opening night
flashes and bangs 126
flats 124-7
flyers 96
food and drink 24, 51, 87
formalities 22
Frog Prince, The 114
front of house 50-1, 120

gauze 126
Genie 74, 104, 113, 138
gesticulation 72, 78
giants and ogres 12, 113
glitter curtains 126
Goldilocks and the Three Bears 114
Goodies 6, 72, 110, 113
Grimaldi, Joe 6, 111
ground rows 126

hair 48
Hansel and Gretel 86, 110, 114
Harlequin 6
health 24
heroine 73, 110, 113,
Hop o' My Thumb 114
House that Jack Built, The 114
humour 13, 14, 16, 20, 58, 75-8, 88, 90, 108, 110-11
Humpty Dumpty 86, 94, 114

improvisation 75 *see also* ad lib
insurance 23
interpretation 18, 58, 105

intonation 73-4

Jack and Jill 114
Jack and the Beanstalk 12, 26, 87, 94, 108, 109, 112-14
Jack, the Giant Killer 114
jewellery 130

King Rat 110, 113,
kings 112-3, 130

Lane, Lupino 6
lanterns 134-6
last night 119
laughter 67, 77, 118
learning lines 14, 17, 18, 25, 49, 57, 58-9, 85, 105, 116, 120
licences 24
lighting angles 134-6
lights and lighting 25, 30, 45-6, 48, 65, 68, 72, 104, 122, 123, 134-6, 137, 138
line rehearsals 64
line-ups 67, 106
lion 112
Lion, the Witch and the Wardrobe, The 115
Little Bo Peep 114
Little Jack Horner 114
Little Red Riding Hood 6, 110, 113, 114
Long John Silver 112

make-up 6, 48, 66, 68, 110, 122, 123, 138-40
make-up plot 139
Man Friday 113
marking the stage 38
masks 71, 104, 110
mind reading 92
model of set 43, 123
Morgiana 113
Mother Goose 108, 110, 113, 114
Mother Hubbard 113, 114
moves 18, 26 , 58, 59, 71-3, 75, 78, 82, 111, *see also* plotting moves
Mrs Crusoe 108, 111
music 10, 19, 26, 28, 53, 64, 79-81, 137
music rehearsals 26, 28, 84

musical director 80
musicians *see* orchestra

Nero , Emperor 6
newcomers 17, 56, 74, 82, 106

Old King Cole 112, 114
on the spot sounds 136
opening night 69, 116-19
openings 66 *see also* beginning
orchestra 80, 137

pace 62, 64, 67, 74-5, 103, 116, 117, 118-19
pairs 16, 19, 21
partners 78 *see also* double acts
party games 77, 88-9, 92
paternal roles 112-13
pauses 62
pep talks 52, 69, 85,
performances 25, 38, 116-19, 140
personal props 40
personal relations 62-4,
perspective 126-8
Peter Pan 86, 110, 115
photographs 67, 86, 94, 99
physique 18
pianist 80-1
Pinocchio 87, 115
planning 22-33, 44, 48, 120, 122
plot 12-14, 103, 104, 129
plotting moves 26, 28, 30, 31, 33, 55
post-play depression 119-20
posters 86, 93, 96-8,
Potter, Beatrix 115
press 82, 86, 93, 94
Prince Charming 109
Princess Badroubaldour 110, 113
principal boy 109 *see also* hero
printed matter 96-101
producer 16 , 27, 36, 52, 60-1, 68, 94, 117, 122-4, 129, 131, 134, 137 *see also* director
production 49, 94, 117-18, 120

programmes 40-1, 86, 87, 93, 98-101
prompt 48-50, 65
prompt copy 38, 137
props 12, 25, 38, 40-3, 65, 68, 76, 122, 123, 130-3, 137
  cues and positions 41, 42
  stocklist 40, 41, 42, 130
publicity 33, 93-102, 120
publicity manager 34, 93-5
Puss in Boots 108, 112-14

Queen of Hearts 108, 114
queens 110, 112, 113, 130
quick changes 126, 130, 131, 139 *see also* costume changes

radio 94
raffles 51,
read-throughs 16
recorded sound 137
rehearsal
  plan 24-7
  schedule 25, 27, 28, 53,
rehearsals 25, 27, 28, 49, 52-70, 86, 93, 106, 134, 139
responsibilities 34-51, 36-7, 117
Robin Hood 109, 111, 112-14
Robinson Crusoe 86, 87, 108, 113, 114,
roles 15, 16, 71,
Rumpelstiltskin 114
run-throughs 25-6, 64, 65

safety 23, 43, 51 *see also* health
scale drawings 30, 123, 126-7
Scaramouch 6
scene changes 38, 65, 68,
scenery *see* sets
scenes 13, 100, 104, 123, 134 *see also* acts
script 8-14, 53, 55, 56, 60-1, 65, 76, 94, 114-15
sets and set design 25, 43-4, 64, 76, 77, 86, 119, 122, 123-9, 130, 131, 137
Seven Dwarfs 113
sex changes 9

Sheriff of Nottingham 111, 113
Simple Simon 111
Sinbad the Sailor 110, 114, 130
singing 79-80, 88, 111
size of cast 9
slapstick 6, 64, 75-6, 90-1, 104, 108, 111
Sleeping Beauty, The 110, 113-14
smoke 138
snow 138
Snow Queen, The 114
Snow White 86, 110, 112-14
Sorcerer 110
sound 30, 46-7, 68, 122, 123, 136-7
special effects 46-7, 64-6, 68, 91, 104, 122, 123, 135-6, 137-8
stage hands 35, 39, 117
stage manager 35, 37, 38, 50, 69, 134, 137
stage planning 33, 44, 56
stage plans 30, 33, 44, 56, 131
stand-ins 84
standard props 132-3
standing still 72, 93
stars 135
stock control 40, 48
story line 12, 70, 104, 114-5
style 8, 122, 129-30, 134
Sultan of Morocco 113

teams 19, 26, 27, 39, 45, 46, 59, 68, 76, 117, 131, 134, 140
technical considerations 10, 25, 122-40, 116
technical rehearsal 68, 124, 131, 134, 137
techniques 58, 70-9,
telephone tree 27, 29, 53
Telestes 6
terminology 56,
Thousand and One Arabian Nights, A 115
throwing things 76-7, 91, 111
tickets 50-1, 93, 95, 98, 99, 100

timing 62, 68, 74-5, 76, 118
Tinder Box, The 114
Tinkerbell 73, 110
Toad of Toad Hall 112, 115
Tom Thumb 115
Tom, the Piper's Son 114
transformation scenes 104, 110, 126, 136, 138
Treasure Island 115
Treasure Spyland 112
Trip, Jack 108

Ugly Sisters 91, 108, 111, 113
Uncle Abanazar 110, 113

venue 11, 23, 25, 27-9, 51, 81, 86, 98, 120
videos 121
Villain *see* Baddies
visibility 45,
voice 18, 58, 73-4, 111
voice projection 18

wardrobe *see* costumes
weather 46
wicked stepmothers 112, 113
Widow Twankey 6, 11
wigs 48
Wind in the Willows, The 115
wings 124-6
Wishee Washee 111
witches 110, 130
Wizard of Oz, The 112, 115
Wolf 6, 110, 113
word count 13
writing scripts 11